How-To Handbook

Teresa Walter

A Publication of the World Language Division

Director of Product Development: Judith M. Bittinger
Executive Editor: Elinor Chamas
Editorial Development: Cindy M. Johnson
Cover Design: Taurins Design Associates
Text Design and Production: Publishing Services
Production and Manufacturing: James W. Gibbons

ISBN 0-201-89522-6

14 15 16 17 18 - CRK - 08 07 06

Contents

They Don't Prepare Me for This

they don't prepare me for this

a sea of faces so different from my
own mirrored image

some so afraid
of my eyes so large
not almond-shaped
like their beautiful mama's

or of a skin so pale
could she be sick, some must be thinking

but prepared or not
I try

take out your math books, I request
in the Queen's English
isn't math a universal language?
but they sit perfectly still

they don't prepare me for this

so I take a math book
with great flourish point and say MATH BOOK!
immediately 33 math books
are produced

I smile in relief
they smile
in relief

they don't prepare me for this

but I'm gonna try
perhaps I could learn Vietnamese,
Cantonese, Mandarin, Farsi, Korean
and Spanish by Christmas

—Mayra Fernández

From *Barrio Teacher,* © 1992.
Reprinted with permission of the author (Laredo Publishers).

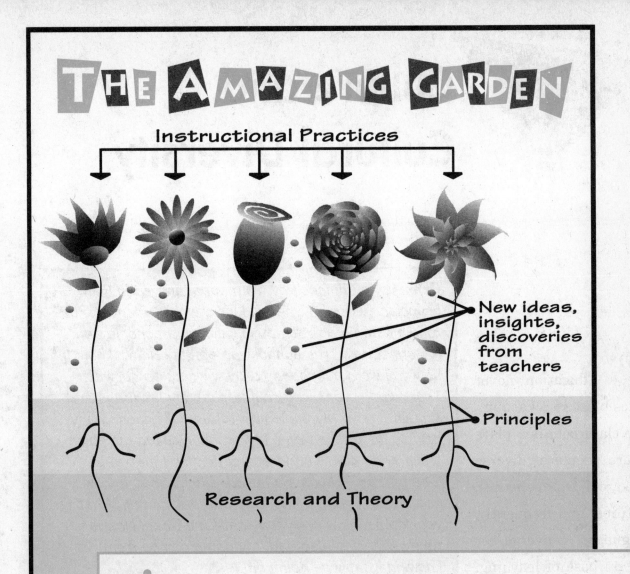

THE AMAZING GARDEN

Instructional Practices

New ideas, insights, discoveries from teachers

Principles

Research and Theory

Skilled teachers are like gardeners, selecting from a vast garden of instructional practices and strategies. The flowers with lasting strength and beauty are those that are rooted in sound principles and grounded in supporting research and theory.

The thoughtful gardener reflects on the garden, which leads to further insights, ideas, and seeds of discovery that take root, influencing and shaping the underlying principles. It is when the foundational levels of principles, research, and theory are understood that the skilled gardener can, with finesse and confidence, pick from the garden the perfect flower that will provide lasting value and beauty. It is then that the skilled teacher can say, "This is the instructional practice I need to use and I understand why."

This handbook is designed for you, the skillful teacher, who wishes to adapt your teaching repertoire to the needs of your diverse classroom. Each chapter presents the most current research about second language acquisition, then presents practical, "how-to" methods for adapting instruction to enhance language acquisition. The handbook is not just for English-as-a-Second Language teachers, but for all educators who wish to address the needs of students whose primary language is other than English.

CHAPTER 1

Culture and Cultural Diversity

Education never takes place in a vacuum. The classroom is a place where people of diverse backgrounds, experiences, cultures, and frequently, languages, converge for the purpose of learning. The dynamics of this interaction can take on many forms, all of which greatly influence schooling. Classroom practices and students' ultimate academic success are largely the result of perceptions of language and culture held by both the teacher and the students (Skutnabb-Kangas, 1984; Cummins, 1984).

The context for learning is influenced both by what students bring with them to school and what we provide in schools. Effective instruction requires that we first know and understand our students, and then use these understandings to create a climate of respect, support, and expectation.

> Dean, 16, a Chinese boy from Laos, arrived in San Francisco when he was 10. Like many students... he remembered his first day in California schools as if it were today. "The school was so big I didn't know how you were supposed to know where to go, when. There was no one who could speak my language and explain to me. My uncle had told me if I needed any help to go to the Dean. My teacher asked me something and I didn't understand her. So I just said, 'Dean. Dean.'—because I needed help. That is how I got my American name. She was asking me, 'What is your name.' Now everybody calls me Dean. Now it is funny, but it is also sad. My name comes from not knowing what was going on."
>
> —Olsen & Chen, The World Enrolls, 1988

Preview: Culture and Cultural Diversity

What do you already KNOW about culture and cultural diversity?

What do you WANT to know or learn?

‘ⓔ Know the Learner

The first step in planning effective instruction is knowing the learner. Gathering background information on students equips the school and teacher to better understand and meet the educational needs of their English learners. We must meet students where they are—and start with what they bring.

Know the Learner

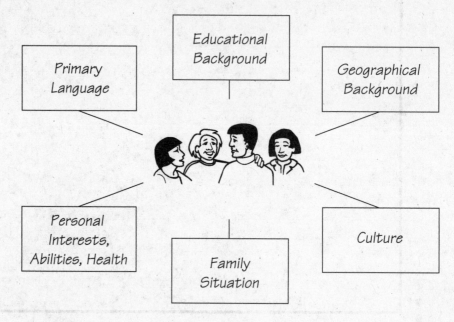

Primary Language

What are the primary languages of your students? What is their level of language proficiency in these languages?

What language or languages are spoken in the home, and in what language does the student function best? In other words, what is the "language of the heart?" Further, to what degree is this primary language developed? Literacy?

Numerous research studies affirm the idea that success and proficiency in one language directly contribute to success and proficiency in another language (Cummins, 1981 1989; Skutnabb-Kangas, 1984; Ramirez, 1992). Identify (and encourage the further development of) the primary language proficiency of students.

Educational Background

How can you help students who have never been in school before? (i.e. develop understanding of school and class procedures such as attendance, lunch, and using the restrooms; teach them to use tools such as scissors, sharpeners, and paint.)

Has the student been in school before? If so, to what degree? Is the child receiving additional supplemental educational services provided by the family?

Students who come to us with high levels of education do better than those who have received little or no prior schooling (Cummins, 1981). Educated students: a) have more academic background, language, and conceptual development that transfers to English; and b) are confident learners who bring an attitude of expectation—they *expect* to learn and succeed.

Students transfer not only their primary language literacy and academic skills, but also their:

- perceptions of themselves as learners,
- coping strategies for how to learn,
- skills at socializing.

(Meyers, 1993)

Geographical Background: Immigrant, Refugee, or Native-born?

What is the country of origin? What are the circumstances of immigration? Was immigration to the United States a conscious choice or necessitated by war or immanent danger or hardship? Was trauma experienced or witnessed prior to or as a part of immigration?

It is normal for immigrants, and refugees in particular, to go through a period of adjustment, or "culture shock," upon arriving in the United States and entering its institutions. Background knowledge about the circumstances of immigration helps the school and teacher understand and be sensitive to the issues faced by the new arrivals as well as be proactive in planning and providing needed support or support services.

What are the circumstances of arrival for your students? Encourage them to share their stories with one another.

Tip Have students develop poster reports that describe and/or picture the place of origin, family, significant events, etc. Students may also bring in significant items or artifacts.

Culture

What is the dominant cultural background of the student/family? What are the basic beliefs concerning education (e.g. attendance, roles and responsibilities of teachers, students, and parents), family, friends, conflict resolution, religious beliefs, etc.? What are the major important days of celebration?

Understanding is based on and begins with respect for and appreciation of individual, family, and cultural diversity. This understanding must extend beyond surface manifestations (holidays, foods, etc.) to the deeper elements of culture such as values and beliefs. Information regarding the background culture of students can be obtained from the students themselves, parents, community organizations and resources, colleagues, and print resources.

What cultures are represented in your class? How can you demonstrate that these cultures are valued and respected?

Refer to "Understanding Culture," page 7.

Family Situation

Is the family intact? Are the parents alive/together/separated? Living with their children? Are the siblings together/separated? Are there other family members/friends living in the home? Does anyone in the home speak English? Is the family in the United States permanently/temporarily? Is the family aware of available community resources and services in their home language/culture?

An awareness of family situations helps teachers better understand their students, and establishes a framework for parent involvement. The context and perceptions children bring with

What are the family situations of your students? How can you use this information to support both the child and his or her family?

What are the special talents and abilities of your students? How can you tie this into classroom instruction across the curriculum? Do your students exhibit signs of potential health concerns? Could vision or hearing problems be interfering with comprehension?

them are rooted in the home. Family factors such as coherence, level of stress, and ability to access mainstream American life via language or other resources, all contribute to a student's ability to successfully function in school.

Personal Interests/Abilities/Health

What are the student's special interests, abilities, or talents? Are there any physical or health conditions that influence learning or instruction (i.e. vision, hearing, food allergies, etc.)?

Using a child's natural interest or skills in a given area serves as an excellent starting point and vehicle for further learning. In addition, it demonstrates to all around that the student is capable, even if the student can not yet give voice to these abilities in English. Additionally, it is not uncommon for refugees or immigrants to bring health conditions that may or may not have been properly diagnosed. Identifying and treating these conditions will make a positive impact on learning and adjusting to a new environment.

Gathering Background Information

HOW TO Gathering the information can be a challenge. Possible resources include parents, former teachers, friends, sponsoring agencies (in the case of many refugees or immigrants), community resources, school files and documents, or the students themselves.

It is most helpful to get the information on the same day the student is enrolled, as the family often brings a interpreter. If not, schedule a parent conference as soon as possible.

As students become more comfortable in the new environment and more competent English users, they become one of the best sources of their own histories.

Tip Use the "Background Information Survey" on page 104 as a tool for gathering this information. If necessary, include additional information on the back of the form.

BRAINSTORM What are some ways that background information will serve a practical purpose in your instruction?

‘☺ Understanding Culture

Culture is the way we do things around here.

—Aida Walqui-van Lier

Children bring with them to the classroom a rich variety of cultural backgrounds. In addressing this diversity, teachers have a two-fold responsibility:

- To try to understand and be sensitive to the diverse cultures students bring with them;

- To help students understand and adjust to the new culture of which they are now a part.

Both of these pieces must be in place for students to feel that what they bring with them is valued and respected, as well as feeling that they fit in and have a place in the new culture. Meaningful appreciation of cultural diversity grows from concrete, positive personal experiences, interactions, and awareness.

Language, that which is used to describe, label, and communicate our world, is intricately tied to culture. Functional aspects of language, such as the meaning given to gestures and body language and the social norms that dictate appropriate language usage, are defined by the culture of the language users. Demonstrating value and respect for an individual's language serves to validate that individual's culture as well.

To be a student of culture, teachers must be patient and observant. Behavior standards are not universal. What is common and expected in one culture may be unacceptable in another. Students who consistently "interrupt" conversations or hesitate to chime in may be reflecting behavioral norms supported by their home cultures. Body language or nonverbal communication is also culturally based. In some cultures, avoiding eye contact is interpreted as being evasive or apathetic—in others, focusing the eyes downward is seen as the utmost form of respect. Sensitivity, respect, and knowledge of different cultural expectations will help teachers gain understanding of the students and families they serve and increase the enjoyment of teaching and living in a culturally diverse environment.

 Tip Consciously model "the way we do things around here." Include procedures, customs, social graces, etc.

How do you provide ongoing *positive* interactions with your students?

 Tip For one day, monitor the nonverbal communication you use in the classroom (i.e. shrugging shoulders, pointing, lifting eyebrows, etc.). Focus on helping your English learners understand what these physical actions mean.

Can you think of behaviors indicating lack of familiarity with American customs or culture, or situations in which students are engaging in behaviors not acceptable in this culture?

 Tip Find times to teach about the expectations of this culture in ways that are respectful, and do not embarrass or degrade. Look for opportunities to develop cultural literacy related to common background knowledge and experiences (i.e. Santa Claus, "The Boy Who Cried Wolf," Mickey Mouse, "The Three Little Pigs," etc.).

What is your personal culture? Beneath each heading
below, list a few items that
signify your own personal culture:

Values and Beliefs

Aspects of Culture

Del Hymes (1974) addresses different aspects of culture, listed below. Add other examples of culture beneath each heading.

Values and Beliefs

- Family
- Success
- Friendship
- Education
- _____
- _____
- _____

Everyday Ways of Doing Things

- Food
- Dress and appearance
- Home routines and chores
- Sense of self and space
- Time and time consciousness
- Rewards and recognition
- _____
- _____
- _____

Special Events

- Holidays and related traditional costumes
- Birthdays
- Religious observations/celebrations
- Other celebrations
- _____
- _____
- _____

Which elements of your personal culture might be difficult
for others to adapt to?

Developing cultural understanding and respect requires us to look beyond *special events* and *everyday ways of doing things* toward *values and beliefs*. It is what is valued and believed, these intangibles, that form the heart of culture.

Building Crosscultural Skills

 Rubin (1975) has identified the following skills as important in building crosscultural skills.

- *Communicate respect*: Transmit, verbally and nonverbally, positive regard, encouragement, and sincere interest.

- *Be non-judgmental*: Withhold judgment and remain objective while listening in such a way that the other can fully share the self.

- *Personalize knowledge and perception*: Recognize and communicate that "my" view or perception may not be the only view or perception.

- *Display empathy*: Try to understand situations from another's point of view. Think, feel, and understand from another's perspective.

- *Role flexibility*: Be able to accomplish tasks in a manner and time frame that accommodates the values and concerns of others.

- *Demonstrate reciprocal concern*: Dialog, interact, and actively engage others in the process at hand.

- *Tolerate ambiguity*: Be able to cope with cultural differences, and new or unpredictable situations with little visible discomfort or irritation.

Where are you in the development of your cross-cultural skills? Review each item in Ruben's list and rank yourself as follows:

√√√ Excellent. "I'm there."

√√ Pretty good. "I'm on the way."

√ Needs work. "Where do I begin?"

BRAINSTORM How can you help students build these crosscultural skills?

I have come to a frightening conclusion. I am the decisive element in the classroom. It is my personal approach that creates the climate. It is my daily mood that makes the weather. As a teacher I possess tremendous power to make a child's life miserable or joyous. I can be a tool of torture or an instrument of inspiration. I can humiliate or humor, hurt or heal. In all situations it is my response that decides whether crisis will be escalated or de-escalated, and a child humanized or dehumanized.

—Dr. Haim Ginott, Between Teacher and Child

Teachers are given a great opportunity to positively impact the lives of children. Day by day, interaction by interaction, teachers can employ crosscultural skills to build a classroom climate of respect, validation, and expectation. This climate directly impacts student success.

When students feel that they have a place, they will learn. Providing appropriate models and engaging students in positive interactions from day one promotes a positive classroom climate. Aida Walqui-van Lier has proposed the following model that illustrates the interplay among the various cultures to which students belong and the climates in which they daily interact.

Cultural Contexts

Each context has its own culture and climate.

Think about your students... What "worlds" do they walk through each day? How different is the culture of your classroom from the school? their family? the immediate community? society at large?

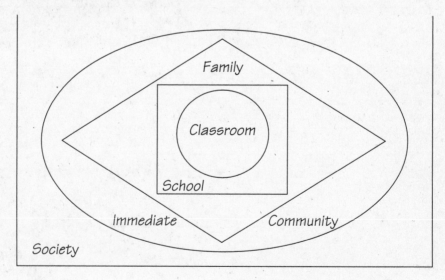

—Adapted from Aida Walqui-van Lier

Each area has its own culture and climate. (For example, the culture of some families may be similar, but each family will have its own unique climate.) It is common for a mismatch to occur from layer to layer. Demonstrating cultural sensitivity and understanding and explicitly acknowledging that "What we do here may be different from..." helps to prepare and equip students to face these inevitable differences. As Aida Walqui-van Lier tells her students, "You must have the strength to face it."

What are the things you do to create a supportive classroom culture and climate that supports students, maintains high expectations, yet recognizes the diverse backgrounds and daily experiences of each student?

‘⊙ The Hidden Curriculum

For children to learn, they need to feel respected and valued. When attention is given to creating a classroom environment and organization where this happens, the conditions for learning are established.

—Leanna Traill

Some of the most powerful factors contributing to classroom climate come from what Leanna Traill calls "The Hidden Curriculum." This hidden curriculum is rarely studied, publicized, or evaluated, yet it pervades all aspects of classroom life and includes:

Reflect on your teaching and classroom climate. Identify your "hidden curriculum" and the ways in which you demonstrate respect and value in:

Attitudes

- *Attitudes*: Knowingly or unknowingly, the attitudes of the teacher are immediately transmitted to students, Teachers must, therefore, actively demonstrate positive attitudes regarding diversity, developing positive self-esteem, encouraging positive interactions, and promoting multi-language use.

Environment

- *Environment*: Everything in the classroom sends a message to students. The environment must be student-centered, recognizing and promoting the languages and cultures students bring with them. Students should feel "at home" in the classroom and see that their work is valued and displayed. Materials reflecting the students' backgrounds should be integral to the room, and furniture should be situated to encourage interaction and use.

Materials

- *Materials*: Materials should include those reflecting the classroom population, and other cultures as well. Students should have access to materials about their countries of origin, immediate communities, and topics of interest, and to the extent possible, resources in their primary language. Students should be encouraged to bring in additional relevant resources.

- *Classroom Organization*: Classroom organization should allow flexibility for varied student interactions (pairs, cooperative/collaborative groups, etc.) and grouping configurations (such as primary language, heterogeneous, and flexible focus groups).

- *Topic Relevance*: Topics should relate to student background, experiences, and immediate needs.

⁑ⓔ Empowerment

One day in Hawaii a ferocious storm washed hundreds of starfish ashore. A woman, on her morning walk, bent down every few steps to throw a starfish back into the sea. A man saw her and commented, "There are so many of the poor things it can't make any real difference for you to throw these few back." With a knowing smile, she tossed another starfish into the water and turning to the man said, "It made a difference to this one."

—Sue Patten Thoele, 1991

It mattered to one...

Reflect and then describe one instance in which *you* made a difference in the life of one student.

The power of individual interactions: James Cummins (1989) has developed a model that demonstrates how educational institutions (schools) can systematically empower or disable English learners. Central to this model is the idea that teachers have the personal power to either empower or disable individual students based on the personal and individual interactions that occur day after day. These interactions, when combined with interactions with others representing the "institutions of society," serve to construct, in the minds of students, a perceived view of themselves as learners, and their place in school and society at large. It is this perception that in effect enables or disables.

Cummins advocates the adoption of principles and practices that serve to empower rather than disable students. These principles and practices are identified below, along with specific implementation strategies and tips.

What have you done that leads to student empowerment? Record your own successes for each category.

Cultural/Language

- *Cultural/Language Incorporation*: The use and development of the primary language is encouraged and supported. Language and culture are viewed as tools to make meaning of content and facilitate learning. Signs, notices, newsletters, etc. incorporate the home language.

- *Home-School Interactions:* Parents are involved as partners and work collaboratively with teachers to provide education in the home and school. Regular home-school communication occurs and parents are invited to observe and participate in classroom and school events.

- *Instructional Practices*: Teachers engage students in tasks that encourage and enable them to become generators of their own knowledge. Instruction is student-centered, with students taking increasing responsibility to interact and use language to express ideas, engage in discourse, negotiate for meaning, and control their own learning.

- *Assessment*: Teachers and schools become advocates for students, seeking to genuinely assist students, rather than using (inappropriate) assessment tools to legitimize the location of the "problem" as being in the student. Student knowledge is assessed in a variety of ways and teachers become "kid watchers," constantly monitoring learning and adapting instruction to match what students need.

The dilemma for many teachers is, "How can I support and validate the languages and cultures of the students in my multi-language classroom when I speak only English?" The answer lies in consciously adopting strategies and practices that empower rather than disable students: know the learner, understand culture and develop crosscultural skills, create a positive classroom climate, and incorporate the empowerment principles and practices described above.

Refer to page 14 for one final list of suggestions for empowering English learners.

Empowering the Learner

Begin with and build on what students *can* do.

Empowering the Language Minority Student in an English Dominant Classroom

- Reflect the various cultural groups in the school district by providing signs in the main office and elsewhere that welcome people in the different languages of the community.

- Encourage students to use the L1 around the school.

- Provide opportunities for students from the same ethnic group to communicate with one another in their L1 where possible (e.g. in cooperative learning groups on at least some occasions).

- Recruit people who can tutor students in their L1.

- Provide books written in the various languages in both classrooms and the school library.

- Incorporate greetings and information in the various languages in newsletters and other official school communications.

- Provide bilingual and/or multilingual signs.

- Display the pictures and objects of the various cultures represented at the school.

- Create units of work that incorporate other languages in addition to the school language.

- Encourage students to write contributions in their L1 for school newspapers and magazines.

- Provide opportunities for students to study their L1 in elective subjects and/or in extracurricular clubs.

- Encourage parents to help in the classroom, library, playground, and in clubs.

- Invite second language learners to use their L1 during assemblies, prize giving, and other official functions.

- Invite people from ethnic minority communities to act as resource people and to speak to students in both formal and informal settings.

From *Empowering Minority Students* by James Cummins, © 1989.
Reprinted by permission.

Promoting Parents as Partners

HOW TO Teachers and parents share similar goals regarding the children they jointly serve. They must, therefore, work as partners to bring together the child's two worlds of home and school, and together help the child learn and grow. Teachers and schools must *initiate* contact and take action to involve parents. Suggestions for parent involvement include:

- Make home visits. Home visits give valuable cultural information, insight, help parents and children feel more comfortable with teacher and school, and give ideas for parent involvement.

- Attend community/cultural celebrations.

- Learn about the traditions and beliefs of parents.

- Trust parents to help at home. The development of ideas, concepts, and processes can be done in any language.

- Conference with parents. Formal and informal conferences provide opportunities for teachers and parents to share information and insights about the student. Provide interpreters.

- Take specific action to involve parents. Invite them. Make personal contacts in the home language. Listen to their ideas and suggestions. Encourage action and be prepared follow their lead.

- Communicate with parents on a regular basis in their home language.

- Expect parents to be involved, and provide the support (interpreters, child care, transportation, etc.) that will enable them to be involved.

Which strategies do you think would be the most effective with your student and parent population?

BRAINSTORM What other specific strategies, activities, or techniques have you used to establish and develop positive home-school connections?

Demonstrating Support for Families

 To demonstrate support for parents, elevate their "status" in the following ways:

- Avoid using children as interpreters for their parents. This shifts the power from parents to children, thereby robbing parents of their parental authority.

- Use parents as cultural and subject matter experts. Invite them as guest speakers to share experiences and/or expertise with the class.

- Encourage the continued development of the primary language in the home. Benefits include the development of language and concepts and continued nurturing and development of important family relationships.

- Understand and be supportive of home culture and family structure, including roles and responsibilities and forms of discipline.

Identifying and Utilizing Community Resources

Most communities have a variety of agencies—both private and public—that serve new immigrants and English learners. Possible community resources include: refugee centers, sponsoring agencies (specific to immigrant population), state and federal relief agencies, churches, private schools, embassies, and key community leaders.

BRAINSTORM What additional resources are available in your school district, community, or city?

THE AMAZING ENGLISH! HOW-TO HANDBOOK

Review: Culture and Cultural Diversity

Refer to and review the preview page for this chapter on page 3.

Was your prior knowledge accurate? (Did you have any misconceptions or inaccurate ideas?)

What did you LEARN about culture and cultural diversity?

How can you apply this information? (Include 1-2 specific ideas.)

What else would you want to know?

Language and Language Acquisition

> Children are seekers of meaning. No sooner do they learn how to talk than they begin asking questions about simple things as well as about the dilemmas of human existence that have perplexed philosophers and theologians from the dawn of time.
>
> —California Department of Education, It's Elementary, 1992

As human beings, we have a need to make meaning of our surroundings. Anyone, when placed in a new situation, immediately tries to sort it out, tying the unknown to the known. This is true for English Language Learners placed in an all-English classroom. They immediately seek out clues to "crack the code" of the classroom. Visuals, gestures, a friendly face, all help students create meaning of the new environment.

It is this need to make meaning that is the heart of language acquisition. As students continue to make and negotiate meaning through relevant interactions and activities, language is acquired at increasingly higher levels. The goal, then, of programs for English language development (ELD) is to use language to communicate effectively and appropriately.

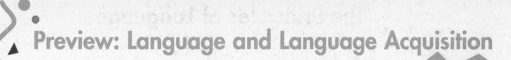

Preview: Language and Language Acquisition

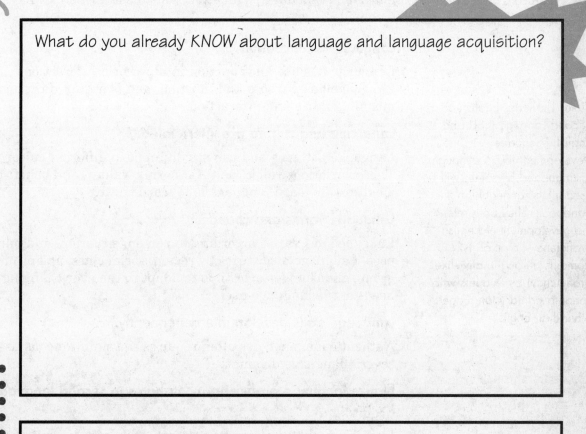

What do you already KNOW about language and language acquisition?

What do you WANT to know or learn?

What is language? Reflect, and then record your own definition of language.

From the abundance of current research in the field of language and language acquisition, some basic principles have emerged:

Language is functional.

Language has use and function in real world interactions. Language has purpose and function, and is acquired through meaningful use and interaction.

Language and culture are interrelated.

Language patterns and use are different in different cultures. These variations reflect cultural norms, values, and beliefs of a culture. To learn language is to learn culture.

Language varies and changes.

Language use varies according to person, situation, and purpose. Language also varies by region, social class, and ethnic group, and changes over time to adapt to the ever-changing needs of the language users.

Language skills develop interdependently.

Authentic language use often requires the simultaneous use of several language domains.

Native language proficiency contributes to second language acquisition.

Proficiency in the native language directly affects one's ability to efficiently acquire both social and academic aspects of a second language.

Note: The terms English as a Second Languge (ESL) and English Language Development (ELD), although distinguished by some, will be used interchangeably in this handbook. They both refer to the development of English proficiency (in all of its domains, through native-like proficiency) by students who speak a primary language other than English.

⊚ Communicative Competence

It is not enough to be able to read, write, and understand basic language. One must be able to use language to get things done. Communicative competence, a term developed by Del Hymes, is defined as the ability to use language appropriately in a variety of contexts. This involves not only employing accurate forms of language, but also knowing the social rules of use that determine what language is appropriate to specific situations (Walqui-van Lier, 1993). Canale (1983) identifies four elements of communicative competence.

Grammatical Competence

This, more than the other competencies, focuses on "correctness" and accuracy. Grammatical competence focuses on the skills necessary to speak and write accurately, or knowing the language "code" (e.g. vocabulary, grammar, pronunciation, spelling, etc.).

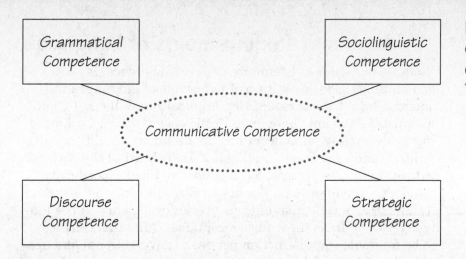

Sociolinguistic Competence

This involves the appropriate use of language in varied social settings. It takes into account factors such as social norms, status of the participants (register), and other rules or social conventions influencing both meaning and form, such as knowing how to request information, accept or refuse assistance, and other "social graces" expected of competent users of the language ("Excuse me, can I borrow your scissors?").

Discourse Competence

Discourse competence is the ability to appropriately engage in conversations requiring the combining and connecting of phrases and sentences. This competence requires the participant to be both a sender and receiver of language, alternating the roles appropriately in conversations or written discourse.

Strategic Competence

This involves the manipulation of language, both verbal and nonverbal, to achieve the communication goals. This competence is utilized for two major reasons:

- To clarify meaning (e.g., paraphrasing an idea, searching for a word, gesturing to convey meaning).

- To enhance communication (e.g., emphasizing a specific word, using body language, or changing voice tone or volume for effect).

Competent users of language must be proficient in appropriately using all aspects of communicative competence. English language development programs should focus on developing all aspects of communicative competence.

If communicative competence is the goal, what types of ESL experiences must students engage in?

Think of one student...What aspects of communicative competence are the most developed? What aspects need more focused attention?

BRAINSTORM How can you model and teach each aspect of communicative competence?

◌ Academic Requirements of Language

Related to the idea of communicative competence, is Cummins's (1984) definition of two levels of language proficiency: Basic Interpersonal Communication Skills (BICS) and Cognitive Academic Language Proficiency (CALP). Cummins notes that many misconceptions about student abilities, capabilities, and even basic intelligence are related to the way in which "language proficiency" has been defined. Specifically, students' conversational fluency in English is often (mistakenly) taken as a reflection of their overall proficiency in the language. To address these misconceptions, Cummins clarifies "the fundamental distinction between conversational and academic aspects of language proficiency" (Cummins, 1984).

BICS This involves using language for social, face-to-face, everyday situations. It tends to be very contextualized, providing abundant clues to comprehension. It refers to basic fluency in the language and is acquired relatively quickly, usually within two years.

CALP This involves language skills and functions of an academic or cognitive nature. This is the language needed to accomplish academic tasks. There are fewer context clues and students must draw meaning from language itself. CALP takes much longer to acquire, about five to seven years.

In school contexts, students must utilize CALP as well as BICS to succeed academically. Students who appear to have achieved native-like conversational skills in English may take several years before they match their native-English speaking peers in academic English. This is largely due to the fact that English speakers are also developing their language proficiency during the same time period. In essence, we're aiming at a moving target and must provide accelerated instruction for students to close the gap.

CALP, however, is highly transferable from one language to another. If you have cognitive proficiency in one language, you simply need to acquire the matching language labels for these ideas in a second language for transfer to occur. This *"Common Underlying Proficiency"* (Cummins, 1981) explains why we don't need to re-learn cognitive or academic tasks such as math and science in a new language.

You May Have Heard

You may have heard teachers at your school saying, "Why does he still need ESL? He speaks English very well. Listen to him on the playground. He talks all the time." When asked how the student is functioning academically, the response is, "He's below grade-level, and not doing well, but the problem must be something other than language." This child has acquired BICS, but not yet achieved CALP, or full proficiency in English. He needs more time for focused academic language development.

BRAINSTORM What evidence have you seen or heard of your students using BICS? CALP?

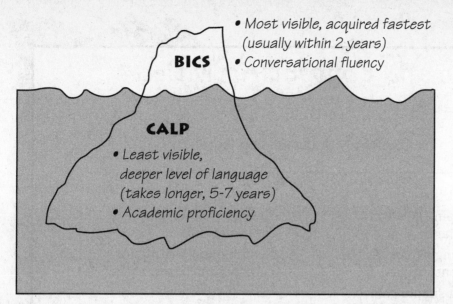

- Most visible, acquired fastest (usually within 2 years)
- Conversational fluency

BICS

CALP

- Least visible, deeper level of language (takes longer, 5-7 years)
- Academic proficiency

BICS and CALP

Think back...Can you think of an instance when a student seemed to be fluent in English, yet had difficulty in the academic areas of the curriculum?

Do you think this was a case in which the child needed more time and focused CALP development? Why do/don't you think this?

Cummins (1981) further defined the dimensions of academic language by looking at tasks along a continuum from context embedded (lots of clues) to context reduced (no context clues). This intersects with tasks ranging from cognitively undemanding (easy) to cognitively demanding (hard). To achieve academically, students must be able to accomplish tasks at all levels. Cummins quadrants are useful in identifying the levels of proficiency required for specific tasks and promoting the use of strategies that help support students in constructing meaning from more academically challenging tasks.

Refer to page 24 for an annotated example of the quadrants.

In which of Cummins's quadrants (on page 24) should instruction begin for students at the earliest stages of language proficiency. Why?

BRAINSTORM What other classroom activities fit into each of Cummins's quadrants?

Language and Content Activities

within Cummins's Quadrants

Cognitively Undemanding (Easy)

Context-Embedded (Clues)

A

- Developing survival vocabulary
- Following demonstrated directions
- Playing simple games
- Engaging in face-to-face interactions
- Participating in art, music, and physical education

C

- Engaging in telephone conversations
- Reading and writing for personal purposes: notes, lists, sketches, etc.

Context-Reduced (No Clues)

B

- Participating in hands-on science and mathematics activities
- Making maps, models, charts, and graphs
- Solving math computational problems
- Making brief oral presentations
- Understanding academic presentations through the use of visuals, demonstrations, active participation, realia, etc.
- Understanding written texts through discussion, illustrations and visuals
- Writing academic reports with the aid of outlines, structures, etc.

D

- Understanding academic presentations without visuals or demonstrations: lectures
- Making formal oral presentations
- Solving math word problems without illustrations
- Writing compositions, essays, and research reports in content areas
- Reading for information in content areas
- Taking standardized achievement texts

Cognitively Demanding (Hard)

—Adapted from Chamot and O'Malley, 1987; Cummins, 1981

How Does the Primary Language Influence the Acquisition of English?

As noted above, knowledge transfers between languages. "The more I know in my primary language, the more I'll know in a new language." It therefore makes a great deal of sense to do everything possible to encourage the development and enrichment of every student's primary language. This can be accomplished in several ways:

Provide Primary Language Instruction

This is particularly important for students in the earlier stages of English language development. Primary language instruction and support in core curricular areas allows students to develop (and "keep up") academically while also investing in their future success in English.

Encourage Primary Language Development at Home

This produces a two-fold benefit:

- Concepts and ideas continue to be developed in the primary language, enriching the primary language and future success in English;

- Parents and children continue to meaningfully communicate over time (Wong-Fillmore, 1991).

Welcome the Use of the Primary Language

Allow opportunities for students to work in primary language clusters to clarify ideas and concepts. Demonstrate that you value the language they bring with them.

The primary language of a child serves as the foundation on which English proficiency is built. *It is never one or the other.* A primary language that is developed and maintained serves to enhance English language development and success in school.

How can you utilize the students' primary language(s) in the classroom?

How else can you promote the development of your students' primary languages?

Building on the Primary Language

Illustration is reprinted from *Teaching to Diversity* by Mary Meyers, © 1993, by permission of Addison-Wesley Publishing Company.

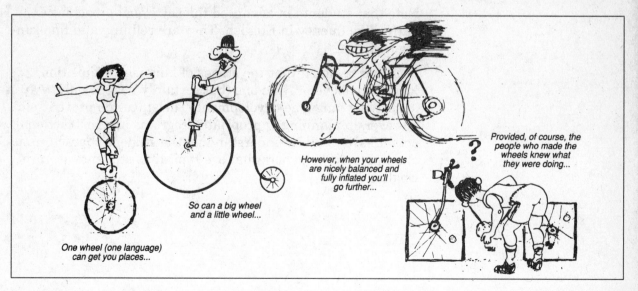

One wheel (one language) can get you places...

So can a big wheel and a little wheel...

However, when your wheels are nicely balanced and fully inflated you'll go further...

Provided, of course, the people who made the wheels knew what they were doing...

The Stages of Language Proficiency

As students acquire a second language, they progress through a series of predictable stages, similar to first language acquisition (Krashen & Terrell, 1983). By interacting with and observing our students, we can identify their stages of language proficiency. This knowledge is combined with what is already known about the students in order to plan appropriate instruction.

Although students progress through the stages in order, they do not always progress at the same rate of speed, nor are each of the stages of equal duration. For example, the preproduction stage typically takes less time than other stages, and the intermediate fluency stage can last a few years. The graph below illustrates the approximate amount of time needed to progress through the stages of language proficiency. Note that these stages refer more to oral language development and that the time frames are very general. Individuals may vary.

Observe your students. In what stages of language proficiency are they?

Is this consistent with their time in English (see graph below)?

What strategies do you use to further language development?

Stages of Language Proficiency

Page 27 describes the stages and instructional strategies appropriate to each.

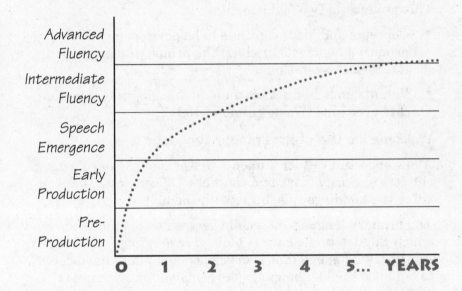

Note that students in advanced fluency are approaching native-like fluency in English. They are refining and fine-tuning their English.

It should be noted that the stages of language acquisition identified above provide one (but certainly not the only) way of identifying language development. The stages do prove useful, however, in planning appropriate programs and instructional activities, as well as understanding the student characteristics and linguistic behaviors that are typical as students acquire English.

Identifying and Developing Language Proficiency

Stage	Students	Teachers
Pre-production	• do not yet produce speech • listen and begin to respond by using nonverbal signals • internalize significant pieces of information • participate through physical actions	• provide comprehensible input/abundant context clues using visuals, realia, manipulatives, gestures, etc. • model all expected behavior • encourage students to follow simple directions involving physical actions • encourage students to join in group songs, chants, recitations, etc. • encourage students to participate in role playing activities • check comprehension frequently
Early Production	• respond with one or two words • attend to hands-on demonstrations with greater comprehension • initiate conversations by pointing and using single words • respond nonverbally to a wider range of language input	• continue to use preproductive stage strategies • use questioning strategies eliciting one or two words such as: **yes/no questions** • descriptive: *Is this a _____?* • predictable: *Will the hen share the bread?* • generalizations: *Does the sun ever shine at night?* • referential: *Did you like the story?* **either/or questions** • *Is this a ____ or a ____?* • *Do you like ___ or ____?* **"WH" questions** • *What color is the ____?* • *When do you get here?*
Speech Emergence	• begin speaking in phrases and short sentences • use speech that sounds telegraphic: "I go home now." • make many errors of grammar and syntax as they experiment with language	• continue to use strategies from earlier stages such as contextualization, modeling, demonstrations, and comprehension checks • model standard language structures • ask questions requiring responses of phrases and short sentences • expand student responses through modeling and expanded conversations • avoid overt error correction
Intermediate Fluency	• respond with a flow of related phrases and sentences • engage in discourse • communicate their thoughts more effectively • engage in everyday conversations without relying on concrete contextual support • begin to develop more academic language	• continue providing comprehensible input and contextualized lessons • utilize SDAIE strategies • ask questions requiring expanded responses • ask more referential questions • *What would you do if ____?* • *What else might happen?*

© 1996, Addison-Wesley Publishing Company, Inc.

⊙ How is Language Acquired?

Research confirms that language acquisition is enhanced when:

Attention is given to background knowledge and experience.

How do you promote language acquisition in your classroom through...

Familiarity

"Familiarity breeds understanding." Tapping into student prior knowledge and experience is a highly effective way of developing understanding, and therefore language. Students connect and apply what they already know to new learning. When requisite background knowledge is lacking, greater time and effort must be spent to build and expand background.

It is also important to note that students with strong educational backgrounds tend to acquire language faster, and at higher levels, than their less educationally advantaged peers (Cummins, 1981). This (primary language) background knowledge transfers to English, making instruction in English more understandable and meaningful.

The context and language are real and purposeful.

Context

Students acquire language when they use it for real purposes. The language used must be relevant, meaningful, and authentic. The focus is always on the functional aspect of language (getting things done) rather than its form (grammatical structures).

As students are actively engaged in what Frank Smith (1988) calls enterprises, they are using language to complete a task, exchange information, or solve a problem that is of interest and relevance to them. The result is both language and cognitive development (Long and Crookes, 1992).

Language is made comprehensible.

Comprehensible Input

Language is acquired when messages are understood (Krashen, 1981; Krashen and Terrell, 1983). Students must understand the intent of the message, not necessarily every word that is spoken. This understanding is not based solely on words. Students also obtain meaning from such things as context, visuals, body language, and real objects and interactions.

Refer to page 32 for tips on providing comprehensible input.

Krashen suggests that language acquisition is the result of receiving these understandable messages, or "comprehensible input." Comprehensible input connects the known to the unknown and enables students to comprehend more than they can produce ("input + 1") actually propelling them to higher levels of language proficiency.

Anxiety is low.

Support

Students acquire language when they are engaged in meaningful activities and their anxiety level is low. The classroom must be a safe and supportive environment in which students feel free to take risks, and recognize that these risks will be rewarded.

THE AMAZING ENGLISH! HOW-TO HANDBOOK

Interaction is high.

A wide range of research affirms the idea that active partici-pation and interaction increases learning (Kagen, 1986; Enright & McCloskey, 1988; Cummins, 1989, 1993; Long, 1982). This is particularly true for language development, as language has function, use, and social interaction as its core. Language must be used to be acquired. Communicative inter-action and the negotiation of meaning between users of the target are essential to the process of acquiring language. Communicative interaction refers to the negotiation of mean-ing through conversations as well as written texts (Cummins, 1993).

Students should be given daily opportunities to use language and interact with a variety of people for a variety of purposes. For example:

- Interacting with a variety of English-speaking models.

- Interacting with large groups, small groups, and partners.

- Interacting with collaborative and cooperative groups.

- Interacting within various language-grouping configura-tions:

    Primary Language: to clarify ideas, concepts, vocabulary.

    English Learner: to modify or "shelter" instruction or pre-view/review a lesson.

    Heterogeneous groups: for cooperative/ collaborative activi-ties, discussions, or learning centers.

Note: The effective language classroom will probably not be a quiet one!

Refer to Chapter 4, page 86 for more information on grouping and collaborative/ cooperative learning.

Krashen's Affective Variables

Krashen (1981) notes three "affective variables" that influence language acquisition:

- *Self-esteem*: Students with high self-esteem view them-selves as capable learners and are more apt to take risks.

- *Motivation*: Motivated students are more focused and take greater risks.

- *Level of Anxiety*: Anxiety inhibits language acquisition. Anxious students tend to focus on form rather than com-munication, and take fewer risks.

Tip Promote self confi-dence by celebrat-ing all attempts at communication and praising specific appropriate behav-iors.

Maintain motivation by pro-viding instruction that is con-sistently academically, linguis-tically, and age-level appropri-ate.

Promote a supportive, nurtur-ing instructional climate. Do not overtly correct grammati-cal or other speech errors. Value the fluency of ideas and comprehension over form.

What Else Influences Language Acquisition?

Personality

Personality traits such as shyness, risk taking behavior, inhibitions, and confidence influence interaction and language acquisition.

Age

Students of all ages can and do acquire language. Current research shows, however, that older children and adults acquire language faster than young children (Collier, 1987; Krashen et al., 1979). This is largely due to the fact that cognitive/academic proficiency is more fully developed in the primary language of older students (Cummins, 1981). Younger pre-adolescent students do have an advantage in one aspect of language acquisition: they are more likely to develop native-like pronunciation skills than their older counterparts.

Attitudes

Student attitudes can affect language acquisition in the following three areas (Richard-Amato, 1988):

- *Attitudes toward self:* This involves self-esteem, self-confidence, and self-perceptions regarding one's ability to learn in general.

- *Attitudes toward language and those who speak it:* This is largely shaped by experiences and interactions with those close by. Negative or positive attitudes (regarding both the first and second language) rub off as a result of first hand experience, or the strong influence of peers or family members.

- *Attitudes toward the teacher and the classroom environment:* This too is largely due to personal or family experiences in school. Positive and negative experiences facilitate the development of strong attitudes that either encourage students to fully participate in the school experience—including acquiring English, the language of school—or create in students a feeling of alienation, leading to ambivalent feelings toward English and education.

Classroom Climate

Refer to Chapter 1, page 10 for more information on classroom climate.

The overall class climate is one that will either enhance or inhibit language acquisition. The classroom must be one in which students feel respected and valued, able to take risks, and free to experiment with language.

THE AMAZING ENGLISH! HOW-TO HANDBOOK

Provide Comprehensible Input

Utilize all the resources at your disposal to make instruction understandable. A list of techniques to help in providing comprehensible input is provided on the next page.

How do you provide comprehensible input?

Use Appropriate Questioning Strategies

Questioning strategies for English learners include using both display and referential questions and matching questions to students' levels of language proficiency.

Display and Referential Questions

Michael Long (1992) describes two basic types of questions used by teachers in the classroom:

- *Display questions:* Questions you already know the answer to that simply display knowledge. What happened first in the story? What is 6 x 5?

  Give personal examples of each type of question.

- *Referential questions:* Questions you don't know the answers to and require students to refer to their own background knowledge or related experiences or opinions. What was your favorite part of the story? How can you show me 6 x 5?

There is a place for both types of questions in the language classroom. (Note, however, that students rarely ask display questions.) Display questions are often asked to check for basic and academic understanding. Referential questions, however, may be more empowering to English learners in that they require students to engage themselves in the language interactions at a higher level.

Self-monitor your questions for one day. Which type do you most often ask? To whom? What are the contexts?

BRAINSTORM How can you incorporate more referential questions while assuring comprehension?

Techniques for Providing Comprehensible Input

- Use visuals, realia, manipulatives, and other concrete materials.
- Use gestures, facial expressions, and body language.
- Modify your speech.
    - Speak clearly, using authentic natural speech.
    - Use shorter, less complex sentences for students in the earlier stages.
    - Use a slightly slower rate of speech—being careful to maintain the natural rhythm and flow of the language.
    - Use longer, but natural, pauses.
    - Use fewer pronouns.
    - Speak clearly and enunciate, using authentic natural language.
    - Use intonation, volume, and pauses to aid meaning.
- Contextualize ideas in relevant, real-life ways, "…just like you did yesterday with…"
- Repeat, rephrase, and/or paraphrase key concepts, directions, etc.
- Model and demonstrate procedures and thought processes through pantomime, role-play, etc.
- Provide only essential information when giving directions.
- Build on what students already know, recognizing and extending approximations of learning and language development.
- Be careful of idioms and slang. Explain them when they occur.
- Clarify meaning in context.
- Encourage participation and interaction.
- Focus on making meaning.
- Maintain a low anxiety level.
- Be enthusiastic!

Matching Questions to Language Proficiency

All students can be encouraged to participate in discussions by varying the questions asked of individuals. Students in earlier stages of language proficiency are asked to point, gesture, or respond with words or phrases. Students with more advanced proficiency are asked questions where the response requires a greater amount of language. Note: This is *not* the same as high level thinking. The key is matching the question to required *speech*, not required thought. Higher level thinking is expected of students at all levels of English language proficiency.

Check for Comprehension/Clarification

Good teachers continually monitor their students' learning and comprehension. Comprehension and clarification checks should be done regularly, using a variety of techniques, such as:

- Students restating the task.

- Students illustrating and/or describing the task and steps involved to a partner.

- Students acting out or role playing directions.

- Teacher asking more "referential" questions, which require comprehension.

(Don't rely on simply asking, "Do you understand?" to which students dutifully nod their heads and smile.)

This ongoing interaction helps teachers monitor progress and identify areas of need or focused attention. (It may be necessary to explicitly teach students how to ask for help or clarification.)

Treat Errors and Grammar Appropriately

Speech and grammatical errors are normal, and even necessary if students are to experiment with and acquire language. How to treat them appropriately is largely dependent on students' level of fluency, educational background, and risk-taking behavior (Diaz-Rico and Weed, 1995).

In the early stages of language proficiency, fluency is much more important than accuracy. Correcting errors leads to anxiety and reduces the student's willingness to speak. Teachers should simply model appropriate language and engage students in conversations. For example, if the child says, "I goed to the park," the teacher responds, "You went to the park! How fun! What did you do?" The student benefits from hearing appropriate forms of language within the context of a real, meaningful conversation. More language is subsequently drawn from students. Focusing on correctness is reserved only

Refer to page 34 for sample questions for each stage.

To effectively utilize this strategy you must know your students' levels of language proficiency. Refer to page 27 for an overview of these levels or stages. Observe your students carefully, asking questions that match and extend their level of English.

What are some of the effective strategies you have used to check comprehension?

When have students fooled you?

Questioning Techniques
for Each Level of the Natural Approach

PREPRODUCTION

(At this level, the questions are more like commands.)

Point to the _____.

Find the _____.

Clap your hands if this is a _____.

Point to your favorite _____.

Put the _____ on the table.

Show me the _____.

EARLY PRODUCTION

Did you like the story? Yes or no?

What color is the giraffe?

What do I have in my hand? (one word response)

Is this hot or cold?

Are these bikes or bats?

SPEECH EMERGENCE

How is the weather today?

Tell me about your _____.

Why? How?

What are you going to buy at the grocery store?

INTERMEDIATE FLUENCY

What do you think of this story?

Compare that with your _____.

What would happen if _____?

Which do you like best? Why?

What would you do if _____?

for times when the meaning is unclear. Again, function (meaning) takes precedence over form.

Older, more proficient students, however, may benefit from instruction related to systematic, or regularly occurring, errors. Random errors need not be overtly corrected (Yorio, 1980).

... probably the best overall strategy is for the teacher to focus on meaning and provide communicative contexts in which students can hear, produce, and learn.

—Diaz-Rico and Weed (1995)

Similarly, regarding grammar:

The effective language teacher, therefore, organizes instruction around meaningful concepts—themes, topics, areas of student interest—and deals with grammar as the need arises. This is done on an individual basis or, when the teacher notices a systematic problem among several students, direct instruction. Practice on the grammar point may be directed to a small group or, when necessary, the class as a whole.

—Diaz-Rico and Weed (1995)

Communicative Context

In early stages of language proficiency, fluency is more important than accuracy.

᎒ Methods for English Language Development

How did you "learn" a foreign language?

What methods were incorporated in the classroom?

How effective were they?

How did you feel?

What did you learn?

Both research and experience demonstrate that a second language is best learned in a manner that approximates how the first language was acquired—by using the language to meet real needs. Thus, second language programs in elementary schools should be designed on a communication-based approach—one which constantly relies on the language as the medium for the exchange of meaningful information and the communication of ideas.

—California Department of Education, It's Elementary, 1992

Developing Language Using Holdaway's Model For Language Learning

Review each step of Holdaway's model. Identify how each is incorporated in a typical ESL activity.

HOW TO Don Holdaway (1986), in researching language acquisition, found that certain conditions related to the acquisition of spoken language were common all over the world. He theorized that these conditions could serve as a model for all language learning. Following are the conditions identified by Holdaway. Although not a method in the true sense, this developmental model serves to identify the conditions and instructional practices that will promote language acquisition and learning in general.

- **Observation of "Demonstrations":** The child observes competent adults that are admired as genuine users of language. The modeled activity is purposeful and authentic. The learner may watch, with no pressure to perform.

- **Participation:** The child is invited to participate because of a genuine need to use language (or master a particular skill). The "expert" welcomes the child while explaining, modeling, and demonstrating what to do. The act becomes collaborative.

- **Role Playing or Practice:** The learner is given an opportunity to practice without observation or direction from the "expert." It is a time to self-monitor, regulate, and assess. The "expert" is nearby if needed.

- **Performance:** When the learner feels ready, he or she shares what has been accomplished and receives approval or acknowledgment.

—Routman (1991)

The following communication-based approaches utilize and combine many of the strategies listed above to create overall approaches for English language development.

THE AMAZING ENGLISH! HOW-TO HANDBOOK

Identifying a Balanced ELD Program

 A well-balanced English Language Development program will be structured around activities or lessons that can be characterized as:

- **Content-based:** using content as the vehicle for language development;

- **Literature-based:** using literature as a tool for language (including literacy) development and enrichment; and

- **Communication-based:** using interactive activities, or language engagement, as a tool for language development. (This technique, in many instances, is similar to the *Task-based* approach, which requires students to *use* language to accomplish a given task or solve a problem (Long and Crookes, 1992).)

Each of these lesson types are important for building the language competence students need for basic communicative as well as academic purposes. In addition, the areas of listening, speaking, reading, writing, and higher-order thinking skills are integrated and woven throughout. It is the integration of all these factors that creates a balanced program leading to both communicative competence and academic success in English.

Identify lessons in your ELD program that are characterized as content, literature, or communication-based.

What is the language focus for each? How are they the same/different?

How do your students benefit from each?

Developing Language Using the Natural Approach

 The Natural Approach, by Tracy Terrell (1981; Krashen & Terrell, 1983), is an application of much current research in the field of language development. Terrell attempted to put into practice what was being learned about natural language acquisition. The basic assumptions underlying the Natural Approach include:

- Language is not explicitly taught but acquired through comprehensible input in a low anxiety environment,

- Language must be meaningful,

- Speech emerges in stages (preproduction—intermediate fluency),

- Second language acquisition is similar to first language acquisition,

- Errors are accepted as developmental, and are treated by providing more comprehensible input.

This method is based on the assumption that speech is not the cause of language acquisition, but the result. Given enough comprehensible input, speech emerges on its own. The primary role of the teacher then, is to provide abundant comprehensible input and engage students in meaningful, relevant activities that encourage the development of language through the stages.

The natural approach is consistent with Holdaway's model. Its focus, however, is to create the language-rich environment in which language develops naturally over time.

Developing Language Using Total Physical Response

 Total Physical Response (TPR) is an approach that is modeled on how children acquire their first language (Asher, 1982). Asher noted three basic elements:

- Listening (and understanding) precedes speaking.

- Understanding is developed through moving the body.

- Speaking is never forced (Diaz-Rico and Weed, 1995).

Using TPR, the teacher gives commands while modeling the corresponding action. For example, the teacher says "Stand up" while standing up, or "Walk to the door" while walking to the door. The commands are repeated and modeled until students respond easily. Gradually, the modeling aspect is removed and students respond when given only the verbal command. The process continues with increasingly more complex commands, and with students taking on the role of teacher and giving commands to others.

This approach is utilized in the initial stages of the Natural Approach and is recommended by Krashen and Terrell (1983) for providing comprehensible input in a low anxiety situation.

> **Tip** The game "Simon Says" is an excellent example of a TPR activity, as are finger-plays and action songs.

Developing Language Using Content-based ESL

> **Tip** Content-based lessons comprise one part of a well-balanced ELD program.

HOW TO This approach utilizes content, or subject-area material, as a vehicle for language acquisition and development. The content is modified to match the language proficiency of the students and is best used within a comprehensive ELD program.

Content-based ELD does not replace content area instruction. In this way, it differs from Specially Designed Academic Instruction in English (SDAIE) or Sheltered English. Content-based ESL has language acquisition as its goal, whereas SDAIE has content mastery as its goal. (Chapter 4 provides further information on SDAIE).

Tools for English Language and Literacy Development

Through literature, they begin to own the new language they are hearing.

—Lapp and Tinajero, 1994

Literature

Literature serves as a rich resource for language and literacy development. Quality literature cultivates language, provides language models, and promotes language acquisition (Lapp and Tinajero, 1994). As students listen to and participate in poems, rhythms, and patterned/predictable books, they experience language that is meaningful and contextualized. Vocabulary, patterns of speech, idioms, and concepts are developed and clarified.

Tip Utilize multicultural literature representing the backgrounds of your students. Encourage students to record the stories of their parents and grandparents to preserve their cultural heritage and use these for further language and literacy development.

Music

Like literature, music serves to enrich and extend language development. Students hear language used in its most lyrical form. There is evidence to show that music (and the language encoded within it) actually enters, and is processed, differently in the brain. This may account for why song lyrics are remembered for years. The pattern and flow of language within a musical context provides opportunities for students to develop language in a non-threatening, meaningful, and fun way.

Tip Display visuals, realia, and sketches or role-play the song to help convey meaning. Students may join in with the music, but it doesn't guarantee comprehension.

Video

When done correctly, carefully selected videos can serve to greatly enhance language and literacy. Videos are a natural tool for language development. They provide a medium in which students can see and hear language that is purposeful, varied, and highly contextualized. Students hear language used for a variety of purposes or functions, and from many different English models. Videos provide abundant context clues from which students draw meaning. Visuals, gestures, auditory clues, actions, and interactions within a purposeful whole all contribute to providing one of the basic tenets of language acquisition—messages that are understandable.

Tip Videos can be incorporated into varied teaching strategies. Refer to Chapter 3, page 64 for information on using videos for a "Directed-Viewing" activity.

Additionally, videos are highly motivating, yet non-threatening. Students usually engage in viewing videos in a comfortable, low-anxiety environment.

Clearly, not all videos are appropriate or valuable for the classroom. Those used must be carefully, and critically selected. A suitable video should be:

- *Complete:* presenting a whole story, idea, or process. Not fragmented pieces of visual or auditory images.

- *Relevant:* relevant to student interests, age, and level of language proficiency.

- *Engaging:* based on authentic works of literature or documentaries that engage students over time with repeated viewings.

- *Brief:* to capture and hold attention, without overburdening students with complex story structure or vocabulary.

To achieve the greatest benefit from viewing a video, students must be active participants. This *active viewing* is accomplished by structuring lessons and utilizing strategies that create a context and purpose for viewing the video and encourage high levels of student interaction.

CD-ROM/Computer Technology

Identify the CD-ROM or other computer programs you have found useful for developing English.

CD-ROM and other computer technology are increasingly important tools for language and literacy development. As technology has allowed "voiced" programs to sound quite human, authentic interaction and meaningful language activities are now available. Programs can be modified and structured to match the specific needs of students.

Communication-based Activities

Effective language acquisition takes place when students have an opportunity to interact and use language for real purposes. In these instances, students are largely unaware of the language processes and structures they are using, but rather, are actively engaged in the activity or task at hand. Communication-based activities are activities around which students can use and acquire language for real purposes.

Visuals, Manipulatives, and Realia

What visuals, manipulatives, and realia do you have immediate access to?

How can you incorporate these resources in daily instruction?

An abundance of resources that can be used to contextualize language, making it visible and tangible, are invaluable tools for the language classroom. Select print materials that are rich in visuals and color. Supplement with magazines, newspaper, or calendar pictures (start a picture file), maps, charts, and models. Provide materials and hands-on activities that will enable students use all of their senses to develop conceptual understanding. Use videos, the overhead projector, the chalkboard, filmstrips, props, and other real objects.

BRAINSTORM What additional resources do you need to create a language-rich classroom?

THE AMAZING ENGLISH! HOW-TO HANDBOOK

Review: Language and Language Acquisition

Refer to and review the preview page for this chapter on page 19.

Was your prior knowledge accurate? (Did you have any misconceptions or inaccurate ideas?)

What did you LEARN about language and language acquisiton?

How can you apply this information? (Include 1-2 specific ideas.)

What else would you want to know?

CHAPTER 3

Literacy Development

Read the following text and then answer the questions in complete sentences.

A krinklejup was parling a tristlebin. A barjam stipped. The barjam grupped "Minto" to the krinklejup. The krinklejup zisked zoely.

1. What was the krinklejup doing?
2. What stipped?
3. What did the barjam grup?
4. How did the krinklejup zisk?

—Gibbons, Learning to Learn in a Second Language, *1993*

Is this reading? Some might argue that this is reading—we could call out the words and answer the questions. This is what many English learners do. They appear to be doing well, they "read" beautifully, answer the questions correctly, yet still have difficulty in many types of literacy activities.

A year-4 English learner (and a fluent reader) was asked the same question—is this reading? His perceptive response:

"Yes, because I could work out the answers." Then he added, "But it's not really reading, because I just went from here," indicating the questions, "to here," indicating the text. "It didn't go through my head." (Gibbons, 1993)

Reading is only reading when *it goes through your head*—when meaning is drawn from print. It is about making meaning. This is true for all students. Students who are learning the English language in all of its domains—listening, speaking, reading, and writing—have more meaning to make.

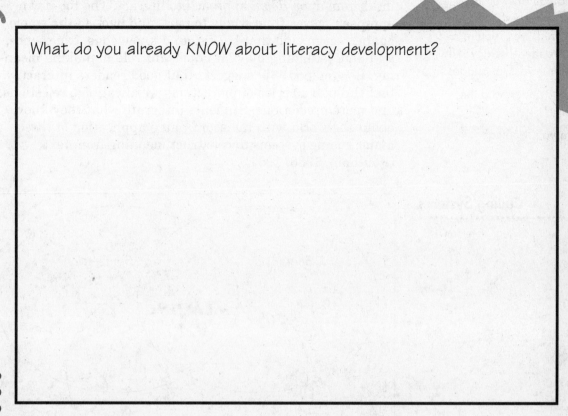

What do you already KNOW about literacy development?

What do you WANT to know or learn?

˙ʘ̈ Making Meaning From Print

Could you answer the questions on page 42? (If you answered "yes" you're a good reader. Literacy skills transfer across languages.)

Did you understand the excerpt?

Were you reading?

Research affirms that English learners, in particular, benefit most from a *top-down* approach to literacy. The top-down approach moves from whole to part, and back to the whole again, recognizing that background knowledge, experience, and understanding play an important role in making meaning. Goodman (1968) suggests that good readers interact with text through a series of predictions, verifications, rejections, and more predictions. Students integrate what they know about the world with the coordinated application of three major cueing systems to construct meaning from text (Routman, 1988, 1991).

Cueing Systems

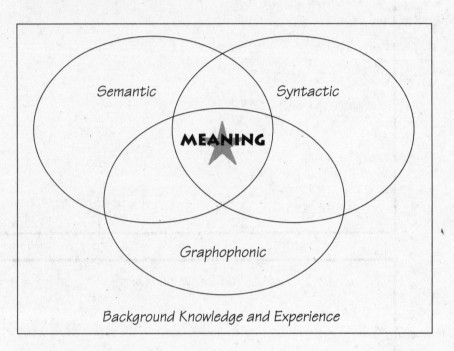

Semantic
Syntactic

MEANING ★

Graphophonic

Background Knowledge and Experience

Semantic: This system focuses on meaning—what is happening. *Does it make sense?*

Syntactic: This system utilizes knowledge of language patterns and grammatical structures. *Does it sound right*

Visual/Graphophonic: This system focuses on sound/symbol relationships and visual aspects of language. *Does it look right?*

Background Knowledge: Although background knowledge is not a cueing system in the strictest sense, it forms the foundation on which the other three cueing systems are based and utilized.

Clearly, all three cueing systems, combined with background knowledge, work together in creating meaning from print. Good readers tend to be flexible, using and integrating the systems interdependently. Developing readers, however, may

THE AMAZING ENGLISH! HOW-TO HANDBOOK

rely too heavily on one system, typically graphophonic cues (Routman, 1988). Each system, used in isolation, presents special challenges for English learners. For example:

Semantic meaning is largely based on shared background and cultural or linguistic knowledge. English learners tend to have gaps in these areas.

Syntactic meaning is based on internalized grammar and linguistic structures. English learners may not have internalized the structures needed to access this system yet.

Visual / Graphophonic meaning is based largely on understanding the verbal connection to written symbols. English contains more meaningful sounds than most other prominent languages. Many English learners will have to learn to first "hear" the sound before they can produce it based on a printed symbol.

English learners, in particular, benefit the most from a balanced literacy program, one in which background knowledge and *all three* cueing systems are utilized and fully developed.

What are some activities you have done that develop each of the cueing systems?

Tip Beware of providing an unbalanced approach to literacy with your English learners.

◌̇◌̈ Promising Practices

The best approach in the instruction of all novice readers and writers is to create a rich environment, steeped in authentic language and stimulating stories that vitally connect with what the children already know and are curious about.

— *California Department of Education,* It's Elementary, *1992*

Conditions For Learning

Brian Cambourne (1988) observed and documented hundreds of children as they were engaged in acquiring literacy. He used this information to identify and develop conditions that promote language acquisition and learning in general. These "conditions" for learning provide an insightful overview of instructional practices that directly affect student learning and language acquisition. They suggest activity to reflect:

Refer to page 47 for tips on using Cambourne's conditions for learning.

Outline ways in which you have used each of Cambourne's conditions in developing language and literacy.

Balanced Literacy

Balanced literacy is the *principled* application of a number of instructional strategies that bring balance to the task of learning to read. The strategies are grounded in beliefs and understandings about how language, and specifically literacy, are acquired and developed. A balanced approach to literacy "combines the language and literature-rich activities associated with whole language with explicit teaching of the skills needed to decode words" (Honig, 1995).

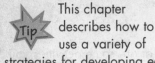
This chapter describes how to use a variety of strategies for developing each of the cueing systems.

After reviewing the strategies, identify the ones you feel are of particular benefit for each cueing system.

A fundamental idea of balanced literacy is that reading and writing are best learned by reading and writing. Students must be engaged in meaningful literacy experiences and enterprises. Through this active engagement, students develop both the personal strategies and the skills that enable them to utilize all cueing systems to draw meaning from increasingly more complex texts.

Balanced literacy promotes a balance between approaches and techniques that serve to develop literacy. Teachers must be skilled in utilizing a variety of strategies and techniques that will guide students along the path of literacy.

Whole Language

Whole language, as a philosophy, promotes the use of any strategy that develops the cueing systems in meaningful ways. This *does* include phonics taught within a meaningful context.

Think back on your language classes. What made it harder or easier for you?

The term "whole language" is difficult to define. It is not just a set of materials, practices, or classroom experiences. It is a philosophy. It is a set of beliefs or guiding principles about teaching and learning on which classroom practices are based. This philosophy is based on current research in language acquisition (Smith, 1971; Chomsky, 1972; K.S. Goodman, 1972, 1974, 1977; Clay, 1977; Krashen, 1977, 1978; Graves, 1978; Holdaway, 1979; Y. Goodman, 1980; Terrell, 1985: in Heald-Taylor, 1991) and is consistent with what we know about second language acquisition.

Ken Goodman (1986) describes practices that make language difficult or easy to learn. Note that they apply equally to second language acquisition and literacy development.

What Makes Language Very Easy or Very Hard to Learn?

It's easy when:	It's hard when:
It's real and natural.	It's artificial.
It's whole.	It's broken into bits and pieces.
It's sensible.	It's nonsense.
It's interesting.	It's dull and uninteresting.
It's relevant.	It's irrelevant to the learner.
It belongs to the learner.	It belongs to somebody else.
It's part of a real event.	It's out of context.
It has social utility.	It has no social value.
It has purpose for the learner.	It has no discernible purpose.
The learner chooses to use it.	It's imposed by someone else.
It's accessible to the learner.	It's inaccessible.
The learner has power to use it.	The learner is powerless.

Cambourne's Conditions for Learning

with Classroom Applications

IMMERSION   Children are surrounded with print.

The classroom is "dripping with print." Environmental print is affixed to walls, doors, and furniture. Student work, stories, charts, and labels are predominant. A comfortable, orderly classroom library invites students to select books. Reading and writing is everywhere!

DEMONSTRATION   Children learn through modeling.

Teachers and students model listening, speaking, reading, and writing through-out the day. Teachers model reading big books or writing using an overhead projector. Students observe literacy used daily in a variety of ways.

EXPECTATION   Students are expected to learn and work at developmentally appropriate tasks.

The classroom is well-supplied with developmentally appropriate materials. Students have materials that match their independent and instructional literacy levels. Centers for listening, art, writing/publishing, computers, math, etc. are available and utilized. The classroom is structured with the expectation of learning.

RESPONSIBILITY   Children share responsibility for their learning.

The classroom is child-centered and structured so students take increasing responsibility for classroom procedures, cleanliness and orderliness, completion of tasks, etc. The teacher serves as informed facilitator, resource, and guide.

EMPLOYMENT   Children are actively engaged in purposeful learning.

Students are engaged in meaningful activities that promote a feeling of owner-ship. They participate in authentic literacy activities such as reading/writing conferences with the teacher and/or peers, process writing, and publishing works. Materials and human resources are utilized to serve this purpose.

APPROXIMATIONS   Children take risks, feel free to experiment, and are celebrated for their efforts.

Instruction and learning is structured so that all students learn and can succeed. Risk-taking behavior is rewarded as approximations to the standard are recognized and celebrated. Students' work is displayed and celebrated.

RESPONSE   Children receive positive and specific feedback.

Activities such as author's chair, conferencing, self-evaluation, and cooperative/collaborative learning provide opportunities for feedback from peers and teachers. This feedback is, in most cases, immediate, specific and constructive.

Conditions reprinted from *The Whole Story: Natural Learning and the Acquisition of Literacy in the Classroom* by Brian Cambourne, © 1988, by permission of Scholastic New Zealand Limited.

Using Whole Language Principles

Yvonne and David Freeman identify seven whole language principles (Freeman, 1992). Following each principle are examples of accompanying classroom practices.

1. **Learning proceeds from whole to part.**

   • Lessons move from the general to the specific.

   • Details are presented within a general conceptual framework.

2. **Lessons should be learner centered because learning is the active construction of knowledge by the students.**

   • There is an attempt to draw on student background knowledge and interests.

   • Students are given choices.

3. **Lessons should have meaning and purpose for students now.**

   • The content is meaningful.

   • It serves a purpose for the learners.

4. **Lessons should engage groups of students in social interactions.**

   • Students work together cooperatively.

   • Student interact with each other as well as the teacher.

5. **Lessons should develop both oral and written language.**

   • Students have opportunities to read and write as well as speak and listen.

6. **Learning should take place in the first language to build concepts and facilitate the acquisition of English.**

   • There is support for the students' first language and culture.

7. **Lessons that show faith in the learner expand students' potential.**

   • The teacher demonstrates a belief and expectation that students will succeed.

—Adapted from Freeman, 1992

HOW TO Using Instructional Strategies to Develop Literacy

The following strategies and techniques are used, modified, and/or combined in a variety of ways to create a balanced literacy program. It is the combining and integrating of the strategies that provides balance and leads to language, and specifically literacy, development.

Note: These strategies are also referred to as "meaning-making" strategies, as they are designed to help students draw meaning from print.

Phonics/Phonemic Awareness

Effective teachers interweave these activities within their instruction and, above all, ensure that phonics teaching is NOT done apart from connected, informative, engaging text.

—Anne Sweet, State of the Art, 1993

Phonemic awareness involves a student's ability to discern the sounds in a word, and then to distinguish between words based on these sounds. Phonics skills, identifying and applying the sound/symbol of written language, emerges from a foundation of phonemic awareness. Phonics and phonemic awareness can be difficult for English learners who are also learning that the sounds that carry meaning in their home language may or may not carry meaning in English. Effective beginning reading instruction for English learners *must* contain a balance of strategies and activities designed to develop English phonemic awareness and phonics within meaningful contexts.

Phonics is an important part of a balanced literacy program. It is the graphophonic cueing system that allows students to verify their reading and decode known, but previously unread, words. Rather than using isolated drills or worksheets that carry little meaning (particularly for English learners who may not know the names of the 10 pictures on the page that are supposed to represent "m"), *phonics strategies are developed and explicitly taught through contextualized reading and writing activities.* These "contextualized" activities are embedded in numerous instructional strategies and approaches, and can take on many forms:

- making alphabet books,
- writing poetry,
- innovations/recreations,
- identifying matching letters and words from a group story or daily news,
- identifying sound or spelling patterns,
- singing and writing lyrics to songs.

Tip Refer to Modeled Writing on page 56. This is an excellent tool for developing phonemic awareness. For example, in writing "The Daily News,"

Teacher: Today is Monday. I will write this sentence. What sounds do you hear in "Today"? (Teacher assists students in listening for the sounds within words, then records the matching letters/words.)

This daily activity is familiar and provides a context for learning.

Tip The following strategies are particularly helpful for developing phonics/phonemic awareness:

- Language Experience (see page 51)
- Guided Reading (see page 54)
- Shared/Modeled Writing (see page 56)
- Developmental Writing (see page 56)
- Recreations and Innovations (see page 66)

As Bobbi Fisher (1995) writes, "...if we as teachers want children to apply their letter and sound knowledge, we must demonstrate how to do this strategically as we read."

As with many activities for English learners, it is appropriate that phonics instruction be made explicit. The context and students' background knowledge must set the stage for focused instruction. Beginning phonics instruction may be developed in the following ways.

Developing Phonemic Awareness

Phonemic awareness begins early. Children benefit from listening to stories and poems, engaging in activities such as fingerplays, songs, clapping-out words, and rhymes that direct their attention to the sounds of language (Willis, 1995). Phonemic awareness continues to develop as students learn the alphabet and develop understanding and skills in phonics.

Learning the Alphabet

This early, important, step can be easily accomplished through song, rhyme, or chants. In addition, abundant and varied activities in which students identify, match, and form letters, as well as alphabet games (e.g., BINGO, computer games, card games) all contribute to learning the alphabet.

Developing Sound and Symbol Awareness

Students who have had many opportunities to hear and play with the alphabet and the sounds of English are better prepared to develop sound/symbol awareness. This process, however, is more complex than it seems. English does not contain a simple one-to-one correspondence between each letter and each sound. English contains many more meaningful sounds (phonemes—about 40) than most languages. In addition, many of these sounds can be represented by many symbols. For example, the "f" sound can be represented by the letters f, ff, or ph (Honig, 1995).

Because of the complexity of the task, many experts recommend beginning with "only the most important and regular of letter-to-sound relationships" and further, that once these relationships are established, "the best way...to refine and extend their knowledge is through repeated opportunities to read" (Law & Eckes, 1990).

For English learners, still learning to make meaning out of the whole sounds of English, it is very important that instruction is embedded in meaningful activities. Activities focusing on encoding (writing) and decoding ("sounding it out") are valuable when a variety of other clues can be drawn from the context as needed.

Remember, whenever possible, it is best that students first learn to read in the language they understand best—their home language. The strategies and skills developed will transfer to reading in English.

Tip Use language English learners have already acquired as tools for developing phonemic awareness. Fully develop the meaning of songs, chants, etc. prior to identifying, or matching, specific sounds within the words.

Tip Use the "Alphabet Song" or the "Alphabet Cheer" for older students. Make alphabet cards for students to hold as they sing. Use alphabet stamps and magnetic letters.

Tip Use a variety of alphabet books to "immerse" students in the sounds of English. Distribute the books, having students look up specific letters. (e.g., "Find the page that includes the first letter of your name.") Discuss and compare the entries for the letter in the various books.

Tip Have students make their own class alphabet (for the wall or a book). Make very large cut-out letters. Assign a student group to each letter and have them illustrate and/or cut from magazines pictures beginning with the sound and paste to the letter cut-out. Arrange and display (or assemble in a book).

The Language Experience Approach

The language experience approach (LEA) is a technique that naturally extends oral language development into reading and writing, using and validating the student's own authentic language. Comprehension and self-esteem are assured because the student's own language serves as the foundation on which literacy is built (McMillan, 1995). This approach has several noted advantages for English learners in particular (Tinajero and Calderon, 1988; Van Allen, 1973; Walter, 1995) as outlined below.

- "Core" reading material is familiar, relevant, and non-threatening, since it is the student's own language.

- The student's language has value and serves to further literacy development.

- The value of life experiences, interests, ideas, and culture are demonstrated both intrinsically and as a source of learning in the classroom.

- The integration of listening, speaking, reading, and writing is demonstrated.

- A shared "background" is assured by the shared experience. It does not assume a single cultural or linguistic background.

- LEA can be modified for students at all stages of language proficiency.

- Conventional use of language (including mechanics) is modeled.

Step by Step: The Language Experience Approach

1. *Share and discuss an experience.* This could be a field trip, science experiment, or literature selection. Allow plenty of time for discussion. This step is crucial in developing key vocabulary and concepts.

2. *Lead the group in dictating a story.* Encourage students to describe the experience. Individuals can contribute words, phrases, and/or sentences. Record the story on chart paper (or overhead/chalkboard). Encourage all students to contribute. The stories can be recorded as:

   - Running Narratives: We went to the park. We walked by many houses.

   - Series of Quotes: Lia said, "I liked the zebra best." Tommy said, "I like the baby giraffe."

3. *Read the story and consider revisions.* Read and discuss the story. Ask students if there are changes, additions, or deletions they want to make. (Younger children will probably like the story as is.) Model and involve students in thinking through these decisions. Make changes as suggested. (Sentences on chart paper can be cut apart and physically reordered.)

 A note on errors: As a general rule, record student's words exactly as they are spoken. However, when speech "errors" occur, ask the child, as if clarifying meaning, "Is this what I should write?" as you model the standard form.

For example:

Student: We goed to the park.

Teacher: Yes, we went to the park. Shall I write, "We went to the park"?

The concern here is to avoid confusing students in the group who have already acquired the irregular grammatical structure of "went." The teacher, the language authority, should be viewed as one who consistently models the standard to which students are aiming.

4. *Read and reread the story.* Lead students in choral reading the story. Continue with echo reading, encouraging individuals or partners to read portions of the story, etc.

5. *Extend the experience.* Use the story to extend literacy and explore aspects of print, with activities such as:

- Students illustrate the story and attach illustrations to the chart.

- Students create a big-book version of the story.

- Copy the story and duplicate for each student. Students illustrate, read, and take home their own copy.

- Explore aspects of print. For example:

  - Students find and/or identify matching words

  - Students identify letters, words, sentences, capitalization, and punctuation.

  - Copy the story on sentence strips. Students match the strips to story sentences and/or order the sentences in story sequence, using the chart story as a visual reference.

  - Make word cards. Students match the card to the word on the story and/or order the word cards to create sentences from the story.

Tip LEA provides good opportunities to develop phonemic awareness, phonics, and other conventions of print.

Read Aloud

Reading aloud allows students to listen and absorb the sounds of language. Selections should be made based on student interests. Reading aloud is a shared pleasure that reaps significant communicative and academic rewards including: vocabulary development, exposure to varied styles and registers of English, and exposure to varied story structures, genres, authors, and illustrators. Reading aloud also fosters a love of reading, demonstrates the connection between the written and spoken word, allows students to vicariously explore emotions and experiences, and contributes to the overall development of communicative competence. Reading aloud has a place in the daily program at all ages.

Reading aloud provides the first-hand experiences that teach students how print works and, even for very young children, serves to nurture a growing awareness and understanding of print (i.e., directionality, print encoding language, formatting of print, and the fact that words are comprised of letters) (Adams and Bruck, 1995).

Shared Reading

Shared reading is based on the bedtime story experience (Holdaway, 1979). It begins with students sitting close together to share a good story, poem, or even a song. In subsequent readings, students are encouraged to join in and read with the teacher, until finally, students can read the text independently. All children are supported and encouraged to construct meaning through illustrations, language patterns, active participation, and enthusiastic reading by the teacher.

Reggie Routman (1991) defines shared reading as "any rewarding reading situation in which a learner or group of learners sees the text, observes an expert reading it with fluency and expression, and is invited to read along."

Step by Step: Shared Reading

1. *Select a high interest text.* It may be above the students' independent reading levels. Select texts that use natural language, provide abundant visual cues, and appeal to children (i.e., the kinds of stories they want to hear again and again). Younger students will benefit from texts that are predictable and/or contain rhythm or rhyme.

2. *Draw children to the selection.* Discuss the title, cover, and cover illustrations. Encourage predictions and tap into background knowledge and related experiences.

3. *Read the selection to students.* Model good use of language and characterization. Emphasize the dramatic qualities of the selection. Read straight through, pausing only for important predictions or comments. Maintain the whole. Do not overly question during the first reading. Keep the reading fun.

4. *Reread the selection.* Read the selection again, encouraging students to read portions of the text with you. Students can also "echo" read—repeat after you, one or two sentences at a time. Reread several times, encouraging participation through reading, role-play, adding sound effects, reading "lines," etc. DO NOT OVERKILL. Stop when interest wanes.

5. *Extend the learning.* Extend the learning with activities matching the interests and needs of your students. For example, make story recreations or innovations, plays, puppets, charts, research projects, murals, content connections, and so on.

Tip Innovations of rhyming or patterned stories provide a good opportunity for developing phonics and phonemic awareness.

Guided Reading

Guided reading is the bridge between shared and independent reading. The teacher guides students to talk, think, and question their way through a text that is slightly above their independent reading level. Attention is given to explicitly developing the cueing systems and concepts of print they are using. The guided reading experience enables students to develop strategies, skills, confidence, and an identity as a reader.

Step by Step: Guided Reading

1. *Select the text.* The text should match students' instructional level.

2. *Draw children to the selection.* Discuss the title, cover, and cover illustrations. Encourage predictions and tap into background knowledge and related experiences.

3. *Picture walk and talk.* Talk students through the selection. Model language and concepts. Encourage students to describe illustrations, or note any details that will help them draw meaning. Encourage them to locate text on the page that may confirm predictions.

4. *Students read the selection.* Students read the text independently, or with partners. Observe and monitor the reading. Adjust instruction to match needs.

5. *Return to the text.* Discuss the story. Encourage students to describe reactions, opinions, and related experiences. Students may reread the selection with partners. Identify the "teachable moments." Select specific skills, concepts of print, or strategies to focus on and develop within the context of the selection (e.g., letter/sound relationships, punctuation, style, and rhyme).

6. *Respond to the text.* Extend the learning with related authentic and developmentally appropriate follow-up activities that balance and integrate language and extend learning.

This guided reading process may also be adapted for older students who are now ready to "use the resources within themselves and the book to gain, maintain, and consider meaning for themselves" (Mooney, 1995). The questioning prompts now focus on the deeper literary elements such as the how and why, story structure, character perspectives, motive, etc.

Refer to page 55 for an overview of Observable Reading Behaviors (Fisette, 1993), in addition to ideas for Reading Conferences and a reading log. (This may be useful for independent reading, and reader's workshop, as well.)

Tip Guided reading provides many opportunities to develop and refine language and language conventions. It is very important to know where your students are, then modify the guided reading experience.

Tip You may want to model the process for beginners. Read the text to and with students. Have them choral read or echo read—repeating after you one or two sentences at a time.

Tip Observe students carefully. Use this opportunity to develop and refine language, cueing strategies, and conventions of print.

Observable Reading Characteristics

General Reading Behaviors

- Chooses an appropriate book: familiar or unfamiliar.
- Exhibits reading-like behavior with no sequential text attention, and uses own language. (Uses picture cues and experiential knowledge.)
- Exhibits reading-like behavior approximating the language of the text. (Print is constant.)
- Exhibits reading-like behavior, approximating the language of the text, and using directional print conventions. (Print carries the message.)
- Tracks print 1:1 with finger or eyes.
- Understands the concept of a letter.
- Understands the concept of a word.
- Locates specific words in text by rereading and confirming with phonological and visual cues.
- Knows some words by sight.
- Uses the cueing systems:
  - semantic cues
  - syntactic cues
  - phonological cues
  - visual cues
- Integrates the cueing systems to gain meaning from text.
- Prepares to read orally by reading silently.

Reading Strategies

- Expects the text to make sense and sound right.
- Reads for meaning—not to identify words.
- Processes chunks of language.
- Make predictions about text.
- Self-corrects when predictions are unsatisfactory. (Cross checks cueing systems.)
- Employs self-correcting strategies when in difficulty:
  - rereads sentence from the beginning.
  - reads on to end of sentence.
  - uses beginning letters or cues.
  - uses picture cues, then guesses.
  - uses phonetic or structural analysis.

Comprehension

- Retells story or passage in own words.
- Talks about the characters.
- Recalls the main idea.
- Recalls the supporting details.
- Understands story sequence.
- Understands story structure.
- Makes inferences about the story and supports them with prior knowledge or evidence from text.

Reading Conference

- *Choosing a book:* "Find a book to read to me that is just right for you, not too hard and not too easy."
- *Beginning of conference:* "While you are reading, I will be listening and writing down all that you show me you know about reading."
- *Comprehension:* "Now tell me all that you remember about the story from beginning to end."

Books I've Read

Name: _____

Title	Date	☺	☻	☹

Reprinted from "Practical Authentic Assessment" by D. Fisette, by permission of *The California Reader*.

Independent Reading

Refer to page 69 for a description of the necessary elements of literacy instruction for English learners. Note that students must have access to materials matching their independent as well as instructional levels.

Independent reading is not a stage to be reached but a part of every stage of reading (Mooney, 1990). Students take responsibility for selecting books and take on the role of reader. It is an integral part of a balanced literacy program where students have an opportunity to self-select books and have access to many and varied books that match their independent reading levels. Students read for the pleasure of reading. Krashen (1993) notes numerous studies that show a direct correlation between "free voluntary reading" and better reading comprehension, writing style, vocabulary, spelling, and grammatical development. Provide opportunities to conference with individual students, as well as allowing them time to share their readings with other students.

Shared/Modeled Writing

Shared writing is an excellent opportunity for developing phonemic awareness and the conventions of writing, including capitalization and punctuation.

Shared or modeled writing allows students to see the teacher as a writer as well as a reader. Shared or modeled writing involves *thinking out loud* as you write. The teacher asks questions that draw on and guide students in utilizing the cueing systems and conventions of print. For example:

- Where do I begin writing?

- What sounds do you hear? What letter comes first?

- What should I write next?

- Do I need a capital letter? question mark?

This explicit demonstration of writing and the strategic use of the three cueing systems can occur daily and in varied contexts, e.g., daily news, chart stories, science observations, math graphing, or note to office.

Emergent/Developmental Writing

Encourage developmental spelling for emergent writers. There is some research that indicates that this helps students develop phonemic awareness.

Students learn to write by writing. Students progress through stages of writing, just as they progress though stages of speech and reading. Teachers must create a classroom environment that encourages emerging writers to experiment and grow. Instructional practices that promote this environment include the following:

- *Value student writing.* Celebrate student attempts at writing—from scribbling, to drawing, to invented spelling, to conventional writing. Focus on what students *can* do.

- *Encourage frequent and varied writing.* Writing across the curriculum should be a daily occurrence. Students can label, list, caption, describe, journal, and create in print.

- *Provide a classroom environment rich in print, literature, and language.* Fill the classroom with student work, environmental print, charts, and books. Encourage students to use language in all of its domains.

Have very beginning students bring in environmental print they can read. Use this to create an "I Can Read" bulletin board or class book.

A Writing Development Case Study

The following case study tracks the progress of one English language learner.

Linh, born in Viet Nam on November 20, 1977, spoke Chinese at home, and although her father was a teacher of schools in Viet Nam, Linh did not attend kindergarten when they arrived in Canada in 1982. In the following year (September 1983), Linh at age 5.9 was placed in a first grade classroom. At the time she was able to speak a few words and simple phrases in English. During the year that the following samples were written (September 1983–November 1984), she received half-hour daily ESL instruction.

In Linh's writing samples we can see how she grappled with the various aspects of writing: creating ideas, symbolic representation, spelling, and the conventions of grammar, punctuation, and capitalization.

The case study and its illustrations are reprinted from *Whole Language Strategies for ESL Students* by Gail Heald-Taylor, © 1991, by permission of Dominie Press.

Linh: Sept. 12, 1983. Age 5.9

9.12.83 In the fall, Linh used scribble to symbolically represent the stories she wrote. Her first scribble had a strong resemblance to Chinese characters, the print she would likely see in her home.

I walking with my friend to play with her. I play the teacher. It fun to play. and my friend. I'm the teacher. My friend is a kid.

Linh Oct. 6, 1983. Age 5.10

10.6.83 Linh's horizontal scribble, written in a left to right motion across the page to describe playing with her friend, indicates that she is aware of the direction of English print.

Literacy Development

My friend went out
trick or treating. She give
me candy. Her name is
Binh. I give her a candy.
Then I go home and give my
sister one candy or two. My
mom come home and said
I can't go out.

Linh Nov. 1, 1983. Age: 5.11

11.1.83 In this sample, Linh has used conventional alphabet letters as well as scribble to symbolically represent her story about Halloween. Although she was aware that conventional letters are used in text, she doesn't know how to use them appropriately.

11.15.83 In this rain story, Linh has represented the text with scribble symbols except for the word "rain-day" which she read and copied from a group chart. It is interesting that in her "reading," "rain-day" was not included as part of the oral translation.

rain-day

I went outside with my
cousin. My cousin's name
Kien. My and my friend
is coming and we go inside
and we had hot water.

Linh Nov. 15, 1983. Age: 5.11

My mom make me a cookie.

Linh: Dec. 1983. Age: 6.0

12.83 By December, Linh had begun to read and included the sight vocabulary she knew in her composition (my, mom, a, I, am). She was also aware of sound symbol relationships and used this knowledge in her consonant spellings (m——— for made, c——— for cookie).

1.5.84 Linh spelled most words accurately in this story and used scribble only as placeholders for parts of words she couldn't spell.

It is fun to go to skating. ~~bwww · cwww fwww~~ I like to go skating

It is fun to go to skating because its' fun. I like to go skating.
Linh: Jan. 5, 1984. Age: 6.1

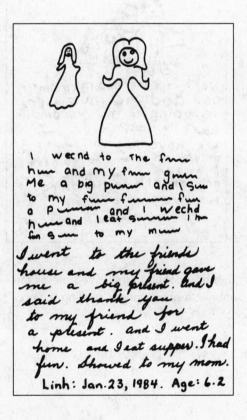

I wecnd to the fww hww and my fww gwww Me a big pwww and I sww to my fww fwwww fww a pwwww and I wechd hww and I eat swwww Ihm fun g ww to my mww

I went to the friends house and my friend gave me a big present. and I said thank you to my friend for a present. and I went home and I eat supper. I had fun. showed to my mom.
Linh: Jan. 23, 1984. Age: 6.2

1.23.84 In this sample, Linh has concentrated on developing the composition. Her story about receiving a present from a friend contains 5 complete thoughts about a single topic. She uses many correct spellings, numerous consonant spellings, and relies on scribble as placeholders for the unknown orthography.

1.30.84 By the end of January, Linh represented her stories with only conventional symbols and ceased to scribble.

I went to the party yesterday and I had fun and I eat Chinese food and I dancing goob!
Linh Jan. 30, 1984. Age: 6.2

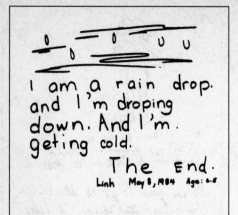

I am a rain drop.
and I'm droping
down. And I'm.
geting cold.
            The End.
    Linh May 8, 1984 Age: 6-5

5.8.84 During the spring, she appeared to be concentrating on spelling, grammar, and punctuation rather than the composition. In this May sample, she has spelled most words correctly, has learned rules of grammar (droping, geting), and has begun to use the period appropriately.

9.28.84 In September, Linh again focused on developing the composition and although the stories lengthened and the spelling had stabilized, there was no evidence of punctuation.

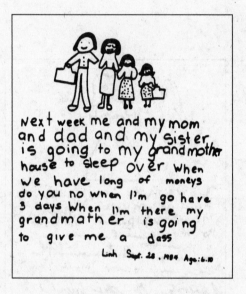

Next week me and my mom
and dad and my sister
is going to my grandmother
house to sleep over When
we have long of moneys
do you no when I'm go have
3 days When I'm there my
grandmather is going
to give me a dess
        Linh Sept. 28, 1984 Age: 6-10

Once a upon a time there were
a farm. And they are eating lunch.
And then the two children went outside
to play. And one of the children
open the door of the cow's door.
And then they went inside. And
then when the door was still open.
And then the cows went out.
And then the little children
went out to play again. And
then they saw the cow was gone.
And then they run. And go
find the cow. And then they went
to the woods. And then they
hear a sound like a cow. And
then they went into the woods
And then they found the cows.
And they went out of the
woods. And then they saw
someone with a light. And
it was the children's mother.
And then they went home.
        Linh Nov. 6, 1984. Age: 6-11

11.6.84 By November, Linh had begun to truly integrate all the conventions of writing: symbolic representation, spelling, composition, and the conventions.

Process Writing

Process writing is an approach that "encourages students to communicate written messages while simultaneously developing their literacy skills in speaking and reading rather than delaying involvement in the writing process..." (Heald-Taylor, 1991). This flexible framework is useful for students at all developmental stages. The five steps, summarized below, can be adapted to meet the needs of individuals and different writing situations. In real life, and the classroom, many types of writing are complete after the first draft. Only selected pieces are fully developed through all five stages.

Step by Step: Process Writing

1. *Prewriting.* Prewriting experiences help students tap into background knowledge and experience, and develop the need and desire to write. They involve students in collecting a resource pool of possible writing ideas, vocabulary, and language structures. These experiences can include a shared field trip, cooking, discussions, brainstorming, creating a graphic organizer, and relating literature.

2. *Drafting.* Children can scribe their thoughts using scribbles, drawings, letters, or more conventional writing. The purpose here is to get ideas and thoughts down on paper. Spelling, mechanics, and structure take a back seat to a fluency of ideas. Students approximate standard language usage.

3. *Sharing and responding to writing.* Students share their writing with a partner, group, or teacher. This can be done informally, collaboratively, or as part of a writer's conference. Students respond to writing in supportive and helpful ways by modeling positive responses and thoughtful questions. A writer's conference may include focused attention on specific skills or strategies.

4. *Revising writing.* Students incorporate feedback from responses and make corrections, additions, or deletions to their writing. This stage concerns itself with both content—the flow and communication of thought—and mechanics.

5. *Publishing.* Publishing is the culmination of a significant work. There are numerous ways in which students can publish their work: posters, charts, letters, and books, be they big books, little books, accordion books, puppet or shape books, pop-up books, or bound books.

Tip Prewriting is a crucial step for English learners. You may spend a great deal of extra time developing the language and planning the writing.

Tip Determine the purpose of students' writing. Use this to determine the degree to which the piece will be taken through the writing process. Do not expect or require all pieces of writing to be letter perfect. English learners, in particular, need opportunities to develop fluency in writing, just as in speech.

How to Make a Hundred Different Book Illustrations

1. Make your story characters from a material in List 1.

2. Add your characters to a background technique from List 2.

   For example: textured bear stickers on a green splatter background; felt marker characters against a wash backdrop.

LIST 1	LIST 2
pictures from magazines	wet paper paint wash
felt markers	splatter printing
students' photographs	marble painting
drawings	dry brush painting
commercial stamps	fingerpainting
silhouettes	Crayola marker with water
stickers	Styrofoam border prints
stencil people and animals	straw blow paintings
children's wallpaper books	sponge painted background
computer graphics	coffee or tea stained
gummed shapes	wallpaper backgrounds
cut or torn paper	glue on tissue paper squares
fingerprint characters	rubbings

_____   _____

_____   _____

_____   _____

_____   _____

_____   _____

_____   _____

From *Teaching to Diversity* by Mary Meyers, © 1993.
Reprinted by permission of Addison-Wesley Publishing Company.

Reader's Workshop

Reader's workshop is an element of a balanced literacy program designed for fluent readers who are working independently, with partners, or with the whole class. Students are engaged in daily reading and interactions with others about the reading. Reader's workshop replicates what "real readers" do: read, reflect, discuss, and respond. The processes and procedures may vary based on student needs and interests (Atwell, 1987; Calkins, 1991; Schell, 1995). Nancie Atwell (1987) identifies three major elements of reader's workshop:

- *Time:* Students are given time to read. The value of reading is demonstrated as time is reserved for independent reading.

- *Ownership:* Students are given choices about their reading. Guidelines may be established, however, and there may be times that the entire class works on the same piece of literature.

- *Response:* Students are given regular opportunities to reflect on and respond to their own, and other's reading.

Step by Step: Reader's Workshop

1. *Mini-Lesson.* A brief (5–10 minute) mini-lesson is presented on a specific aspect of reading.

2. *Students read.* Students read independently, with partners, or in small groups. The teacher may be reading or conferencing, responding to journals, holding book talks, etc.

3. *Writing journal entries.* Students write an entry in their reading journal about the reading. (Students label each entry with the date, title, and page number.) Rather than a retelling, the entry should foster a discussion about the book by making or verifying predictions, ponderings, or relating similar experiences. Students share their thoughts, feelings, concerns, and questions about the story, characters, author, etc.

4. *Responding to reading journal.* Students are paired (or may work in small groups) and read each other's journal entry. They may be reading the same or different books. Students write a response to the entry on the journal page itself. This dialog is continued through the reading of the entire book.

5. *Book Log.* Completed books are listed on a book log.

Writer's Workshop

Writer's workshop is similar in philosophy and purpose to reader's workshop. Elements of writer's workshop include time, ownership, response, and identifying writing role models (Atwell, 1987). Students are engaged in daily writing, for varied purposes, and participate regularly in writing conferences with peers and the teacher (Atwell, 1987; Calkins, 1991; Schell, 1995).

Step by Step: Writer's Workshop

1. *Mini-Lesson.* A brief (5–10 minute) mini-lesson is presented on a specific aspect of writing.

2. *Status of the class.* The teacher briefly "checks-in" with each student to determine the project (what they are writing) and the stage they're working on (draft, revision, etc.). The teacher records this information on a "monitoring chart" to provide accountability and assess student needs.

3. *Students write.* Students work on their project. They may be at any stage of the process from prewriting to publishing.

4. *Conferencing.* As students write, the teacher conferences with a few students daily to discuss, monitor, and evaluate writing, and to help students identify their personal positions/perceptions as writers.

5. *Sharing Circle/Author's Chair.* Students share their completed writing with a group or the class.

Directed Reading-Thinking Activities

Directed reading-thinking activities are used to guide and coach students to draw meaning from print as they read segments of the text and respond to predicting and verifying questions. This process replicates, as closely as possible, the way the mind processes text (Treadway, 1989, 1995). The goal of directed reading-thinking is to make explicit the connection between print and meaning and to help students develop meaning-making strategies. Directed reading-thinking is an important tool for selected pieces of literature, but should be used sparingly. It complements strategies in which students routinely read and hear whole works straight through. The process can be used either by reading to students or having students read independently or with partners.

Step by Step: Directed Reading-Thinking Activities

1. *Prepare the text.* Pre-read the text and identify the segments that contain the major events of the story. Try to divide the story into segments that will promote deeper-level thought.

2. *Prepare the students.* Prepare students prior to reading the text by developing background concepts and language. Show the book cover and/or read the title. Encourage students to describe the cover and predict what the story will be about. Ask predicting questions such as:

   - What do you think this story will be about?

   - What characters do you think will be in the story? Why do you think this? Be specific. Record predictions for later reference.

3. *Read a segment of the text.* Read the first story segment. Have students compare their predictions to the actual reading passage in order to either verify their predictions or identify the parts of their predictions that were inaccurate or are still unknown. For example:

   - Were we right about the story/characters?

   - Do we know yet?

4. *Repeat and continue the process.* Ask more predicting questions based on the reading. Record the predictions. Read the next segment. Ask verifying questions.

5. *Review and reread the whole story.* After completing the story, discuss the predictions, reactions, and impressions. Read or have students reread the story as a whole.

Tip Do not use this strategy with every piece of reading. It is also important that students hear stories straight through, as a whole. Select reading pieces that can be presented in short segments and lend themselves to predictions.

Directed Viewing-Thinking

The directed reading-thinking procedure can be adapted for use with videos. The purpose is the same, drawing meaning from and interacting with the story. Follow the steps above, pausing the video to verify and predict.

Identify videos that would lend themselves to this directed viewing-thinking strategy.

Journals and Learning Logs

Journals and learning logs are places where students record what they are pondering and learning in and out of school. In them, students may make sketches, drawings, and notes; record observations and reflections; and interact through print with the teacher or peers. Journals and learning logs allow students to clarify and record ideas for later use.

Interactive journals allow a running dialog with the teacher or peer. Comments written by the teacher in an interactive journal should be authentic, specific, and brief.

Tip Encourage all students to write in their journals on a daily basis.

Reproductions

Reproductions are student-produced pieces of writing that reproduce the exact text of a literature selection. Reproduced stories use the language of the original story, with students providing their own illustrations. Reproductions allow students to internalize the language of the selection and extend it in artistic or symbolic ways. The language remains understandable and readable.

Innovations

Innovations are writings that are both inspired by and maintain the basic structure, pattern, rhythm, or topic of a selection, but give it a new twist. Students may change any element of the story, poem, or song to make it their own. For example, students may make innovations titled: *Marco, Marco, Who do You See? Five Little Froggies Croaking on a Log*, or *Mama's Taking Us To the Beach Tomorrow*. Innovations provide rich opportunities for language and concept expansion. In addition, cueing systems are utilized and developed within meaningful contexts.

Story Mapping

Story mapping can take on several forms. In each case, significant elements of stories are identified and organized in a visual format. Story maps range from literal illustrations or descriptions of important elements to symbolic representations of these elements. Story maps may be completed individually, with partners, or in collaborative groups. It is always interesting to see how individuals or groups will interpret and represent the same story. Several story maps are described below.

Story Reporting Map

These story maps include specific bits of information that students must identify or report about the story. Typical elements

Use the template on page 106 to brainstorm ideas for new content, titles, storylines, and characters for a favorite literary selection.

Tip Use reproductions as an art lesson to replicate the artistic style or techniques of the illustrator. For example, use collage with stories by Eric Carle or Leo Lionni.

Tip Story mapping serves to develop deeper, less tangible literacy skills, such as plot, characterization, imagery, allusion, and perspective.

STORY REPORTING MAP

STORY TITLE		
Characters	Setting	Problem
Beginning	Middle	End

THE AMAZING ENGLISH! HOW-TO HANDBOOK

might include characters, setting, problem, sequence, and solution.

Simple Retelling

Simple retellings involve students in identifying the five to seven major events in a story, and illustrating each. The illustrations are matched to text (summaries of the events) and compiled in a book, or wall story. Guide students in identifying the sequence by first identifying beginning, middle, and end. Next ask what happened between the beginning and middle, and middle and end for five events.

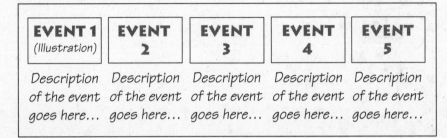

Excitement Map

Excitement maps are extensions of a simple retelling. Students first illustrate, on small pieces of paper, the events of the simple retelling. Next, on chart paper, they draw a graph. The events are written sequentially along the horizontal axis. The vertical column is numbered 1-10. Students select the most exciting part of the story and place it above the matching text at the "ten" at the top of the chart. They continue ranking the remaining events accordingly. The completed map visually demonstrates the building excitement and climax of the story. (Note: Individuals or groups may map their stories differently. Encourage them to justify their work.)

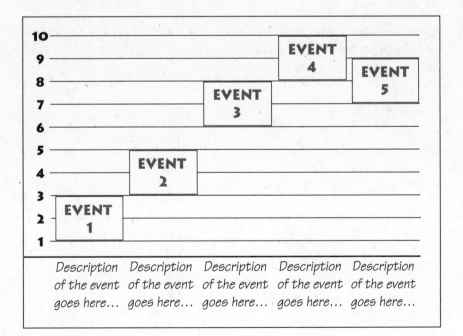

Actual Map

Actual maps are story maps that identify and "locate" the various places that make up the setting or settings of a story. Students illustrate the beginning and continue by drawing a path leading to other places where the action occurred. The events are connected by the path. The direction and shape of the path are determined by the student. Students then add details such as characters and significant items, and label the items on the map (Johnson, 1987).

ACTUAL MAP

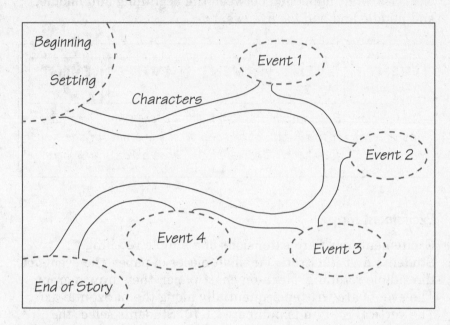

Symbolic Map

Symbolic maps use symbols and illustrations to represent the significant elements of a story. Words are not used to label, but to symbolize or represent ideas. Students represent the key elements of the story in such a way that they can be used to retell the story.

Chapter 4 identifies and describes additional graphic organizers that can be used to develop literature and literacy.

SYMBOLIC MAP

THE AMAZING ENGLISH! HOW-TO HANDBOOK

Tools for Literacy Development

Tools such as literature, music, videos, CD-ROM and other computer technology can be used to develop, extend and enrich language and literacy. Refer to Chapter 2, page 39 for "Tools for Language and Literacy Development."

Connecting with English Language Learners

English language learners who are acquiring literacy in English need experiences and focused instruction for varied purposes. The following diagram describes needed program components (levels of literature and materials) and corresponding strategies (adapted from Bogomaz, 1995).

Essential Components of a Language Arts Program for English Language Learners

1. Independent Reading

Students read independently. Selections are based on what students can read without assistance.

- Sustained Silent Reading (SSR)
- Reader's Workshop

2. Instructional/Developmental Level Reading

Students read with the teacher. The selections are a bit beyond the student's independent reading level. The teacher uses strategies that move students forward in literacy development.

- Read Aloud
- Language Experience Approach (LEA)
- Shared Reading
- Guided Reading

3. Age/Grade Appropriate Literature

Students read with the teacher and/or class (or teacher may read to student). The selections may extend beyond the student's independent and instructional levels. The teacher uses strategies for age/grade level concept and language development.

- Read Aloud
- LEA
- Core literature or district adopted literature materials using specialized strategies
- Shared Reading

The following chart identifies some of the language and literacy development strategies that are particularly helpful for students at each of the specified levels of English language proficiency.

Language Arts Activities Through the Stages

Preproduction/Early Production

- Shared reading
- Concepts about print
- Read aloud, listening post
- SSR
- Choral/Echo reading
- Dramatization/Role play
- Puppetry
- Flannel board stories
- Recreations
- Interactive journals
- Language Experience Approach

Speech Emergence

- Guided reading
- Story mapping
- Reader's theater
- Innovations
- Process writing (emphasis on prewriting/drafting)
- Continue all strategies introduced in earlier stages.

Intermediate/Advanced Fluency

- Process writing (all steps)
- Journal writing
- Reader's workshop
- Writer's workshop
- Directed reading
- Research projects
- Creative dramatics
- Public speaking/formal presentations
- Use of scaffolding to allow access to grade level/age appropriate narrative and expository texts
- Continue with (modified—enriched) strategies previously introduced.

—*Adapted from Bogomaz, 1995*

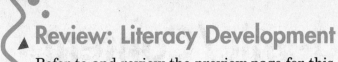

▲ Review: Literacy Development

Refer to and review the preview page for this chapter on page 43.

Was your prior knowledge accurate? (Did you have any misconceptions or inaccurate ideas?)

What did you LEARN about literacy development?

How can you apply this information? (Include 1-2 specific ideas.)

What else would you want to know?

Academic/Content Area Development

It has been noted that we—as educators—require something of English learners that is not required, or even expected, of native-English speakers; that is, that English learners learn a second language to the level that they are able function and do high-level academic work in that new language. Further, the expectation for virtually all English learners is that this be accomplished in a relatively short period of time.

The task is daunting. It is clear that English learners must acquire high levels of English in addition to developing the academic knowledge and skills that will enable them to succeed in school. The question of how to provide access to and further develop the academic or content area curriculum for English learners is the focus of this chapter.

▲ Preview: Academic/Content Area Development

What do you already KNOW about academic/content area development?

What do you WANT to know or learn?

ᐧⓄ Focus on the Learner

Students come to our classes with varied backgrounds, cultures, languages, and ways of learning. All instruction begins with the student. The needs of the student determine the starting point, as well as strategies and approaches that will best promote learning across the curriculum. Using this *student-centered approach,* teachers should consider many factors in determining how students learn best, then apply this information to classroom practices.

Learning Styles/Multiple Intelligences

Learning styles are the preferred ways in which an individual receives and processes information (Meyers, 1993). Students come to us with diverse styles of learning. These have traditionally been identified as visual, auditory, and kinesthetic. The work of Howard Gardner (1985) has extended this idea to encompass the notion of intelligence, or rather "intelligences." Rather than one, overriding intelligence, he believes that people have various areas of intelligence that can develop over time. These intelligences shape how one learns and demonstrates knowledge.

Gardner explains that although each identified intelligence is autonomous, he affirms that intelligences work in harmony. Accomplishing tasks and solving problems typically requires the orchestrated application of several intelligences. Gardner further explains that although these intelligences are demonstrated in a wide variety of cultures, they may manifest themselves differently in different cultures (Haggerty, 1996). How, or whether, an intelligence surfaces in an individual depends on at least two factors (Haggerty, 1996):

1. the biological predisposition to find or solve problems in a given domain, and

2. whether the individual's culture elicits that predisposition or nurtures that domain.

Focusing on and giving students time to nurture and develop their own intelligences results in students who are more apt to discover their own strengths, put more effort into improving their weak areas, and feel better about themselves (Nelson, 1995). If we can identify, appreciate, and provide learning opportunities that appeal to a variety of styles, or "intelligences," we will go far to nurture intelligences and help students learn in ways that are the most meaningful to them.

Refer to pages 75 and 76. Review the descriptions for each intelligence and determine your stronger intelligences. Then answer the following:

How have these intelligences helped you in school?

How were these intelligences nurtured, encouraged, or rewarded?

How could teachers have tapped into these intelligences to help you learn?

How can you use this information to help all students learn?

How to Identify and Nurture Multiple Intelligences: Many Ways to Be Smart!

LINGUISTIC

Sensitivity to words: their meaning, order, sounds, rhythm, and function. This intelligence is required of writers, orators, and those who appreciate them.

Focus on words—on saying them, hearing them and using them. Provide opportunities for discussion, many and varied reading and writing tasks, and oral presentations. Encourage the use of storyboards, tape recorders, computers. Visit libraries, bookstores, newspapers, publishers, and printers.

MUSICAL

Sensitivity to pitch, rhythm, timbre, and the qualities of tone. This intelligence is required of composers, singers, conductors, and those who appreciate them.

Focus on rhythm, melody, and tone. Provide opportunities to listen to and create music, play musical instruments, sing, compose, and dance. Attend concerts, musicals, music demonstrations, and visit recording studios.

LOGICAL-MATHEMATICAL

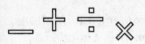

Ability to discern logical or numerical patterns, develop extended chains of reasoning, or handle increasingly abstract tiers of analysis. This intelligence is required of mathematicians, scientists, computer programmers, and individuals involved in finance-related businesses.

Focus on concept formation and finding relationships and patterns. Provide opportunities for experimentation, exploration, classification, categorization, and computer programming. Use games requiring strategy and logical analysis. Use science kits and lab materials. Visit museums of natural science, computer exhibits, banks, accounting firms.

SPATIAL

Capacity to perceive forms and objects accurately, manipulate or mentally transform objects, or form mental images. Spatial intelligence is required of physicists, engineers, architects, artists, mechanics, and chess players.

Focus on images, pictures, color. Encourage visualization of problems. Provide opportunities for drawing, painting, and sculpting. Utilize multimedia, visuals, and realia. Visit art museums, planetariums, and architectural landmarks.

continued on next page

BODILY-KINESTHETIC

Ability to handle objects and one's own body skillfully for functional or expressive purposes. This intelligence is demonstrated by skilled dancers, athletes, actors, surgeons, pianists, violinists, and other skilled craftspersons.

Focus on touching/manipulating objects, bodily movement. Provide opportunities for dramatization, pantomime, and other physical activities. Use playground and gymnasium equipment. Encourage hands-on arts and craft activities. Visit campgrounds, art exhibits, and craft shows. Attend theatrical and dance presentations, and sporting events.

INDIVIDUAL (INTRAPERSONAL)

Ability to understand oneself, including desires, goals, strengths and weaknesses and then act on this understanding. Individual intelligence is required to make appropriate life decisions.

Provide long-term meaningful projects. Encourage students to monitor and reflect on their own learning and explore their own interests and abilities. Give students choices in selecting and using materials. Encourage the use of portfolios.

SOCIAL (INTERPERSONAL)

Ability to distinguish moods, temperament, motivations, and intentions of others and to act on this knowledge. This intelligence is required of those who try to persuade others, such as political or religious leaders, managers, supervisors, counselors, teachers, and parents.

Encourage collaboration and interactions. Provide opportunities for group discussions, group problem solving, collaborative/cooperative projects and products, and peer teaching.

From *Nurturing Multiple Intelligences: A Guide to Multiple Intelligence Theory and Teaching*, by Brian Haggerty, © 1995. Reprinted by permission of Addison-Wesley Publishing Company.

⊙ Accessing Core Curriculum

There are three basic ways of helping English language learners access core content-area curriculum. Ideally, each has its place and all work together to achieve the goal of academic success. The three basic modes are:

Primary Language Instruction

This is most important for students at the earliest stages of English language development, and when developed and maintained, results in fully proficient bilingual students.

Specially Designed Academic Instruction in English (SDAIE)

Also referred to as Sheltered English, this is grade-level instruction in English that utilizes specialized strategies to achieve understanding. SDAIE is best suited for students who have achieved intermediate fluency in English, serving as the bridge between primary language instruction and mainstream instruction in English. However, SDAIE strategies also help provide access to grade-level curriculum for students of varying primary languages and English-proficiency levels who are not able to participate in primary language instruction.

Mainstream (Grade-Level) Classroom Instruction

This is the goal for all students, and is appropriate for students who have achieved full proficiency in English and no longer need additional language support.

Each type of instruction serves a role in the well-designed, fully-equipped program. In fact, many view these three modes as a progression beginning with primary language instruction, then SDAIE, and finally mainstream instruction in English. This chapter will focus on SDAIE—utilizing strategies that make core curriculum accessible to English learners who are learning in English.

⚓ₒᵂ ᵀₒ Providing Specially Designed Academic Instruction in English

SDAIE, also referred to as Sheltered English, is an approach to teaching content curriculum that provides students with extra language and academic support, rather than placing students in an all-English content course and expecting them to either "sink or swim." This extra support enables English learners to access the core concepts and skills of the subject.

SDAIE instruction is provided in English, and combines the principles of second language acquisition with elements of

How does your school provide for:

Primary Language Instruction?

SDAIE?

Mainstream Instruction?

Note: There has been a great deal of discussion regarding the terms "Sheltered English" and SDAIE. For the purposes of this handbook, the terms will be used interchangeably.

good teaching that make the content comprehensible to students (Sobul, 1994). SDAIE instruction involves the careful selection of materials and resources as well as the skillful application of teaching strategies and techniques that will provide access to content by all students.

The central goal of SDAIE is to provide access to grade-level content-related curriculum. Along with this, however, SDAIE also serves to further develop English language proficiency (particularly academic language proficiency), higher-level thinking skills, and advanced literacy skills (Law & Eckes, 1990).

SDAIE is most effective when students have acquired a strong foundation of English (intermediate fluency) and then use this linguistic foundation to develop academic language and concepts in English. Some, in fact, define SDAIE only in these terms. However, the reality of many schools is that students with varying primary languages are placed in English classrooms at all stages of English proficiency. The reasons for this vary, but the situation exists nevertheless. The strategies and approaches utilized in SDAIE will also be effective in helping to provide access to core curriculum for English learners in the multilingual classroom who are unable to obtain primary language instruction in the content areas.

Materials for SDAIE

How to Select

Review the materials you use for one content area, then answer the following:

How do you supplement to promote meaning and provide extra clues for English learners?

How do your materials rate in terms of:

Comprehensibility?

Quality?

Appeal?

Learning grade-level core curriculum is the primary goal of SDAIE. This does not mean, however, that the same materials must be used to accomplish this goal. English learners will benefit most from materials that are selected to promote meaning by providing extra clues through appropriate and abundant visuals, diagrams, and text supports, such as captions, labels, etc. Additionally, teachers may enrich instruction with supplemental materials including maps, visuals of all sorts, newspaper and magazine articles, graphic organizers, videos, audio tapes, and computer programs.

Criteria for selection should include:

- *Comprehensibility*. Are the materials comprehensible to English Learners?

- *Quality Content*. Does the content meet the course objectives? Is it up to date and of the same high quality required for all students?

- *Appeal*. Does the material appeal to the age and interests of the students? Will it appeal to a variety of learning styles? Is the material visually appealing?

Modification

Most materials will need some modification for the SDAIE classroom. The goal of modifying the material (or text) is to increase comprehensibility without watering down the content (Diaz-Rico and Weed, 1995). The following examples, from Amato and Snow (1992 via Diaz-Rico and Weed, 1995, p.122), demonstrate how the techniques of simplification, expansion, and direct definition can aid comprehension:

How have you successfully modified content material for your English learners?

- *Simplification.* "The government's funds were depleted. It was almost out of money."

- *Expansion of Ideas.* "The government's funds were depleted. It had spent a lot of money on many things: guns, equipment, help for the poor. It did not have any more money to spend on anything else."

- *Direct Definition.* "The government's funds were depleted. This means that the government spent all of its money."

Additional modifications might include rewriting paragraphs to follow a consistent structure. For example:

- main ideas followed by supporting details, and

- use of linguistic markers such as:

     first, next, then for sequence,

     because for cause and effect,

     but or *however* for contrast.

These modifications increase readability. As student proficiency increases, so does the complexity of the reading. The purpose is to move students toward working with unmodified texts (Diaz-Rico and Weed, 1995).

Additional material modifications might include:

- using advanced and graphic organizers,

- paraphrasing text rather than reading,

- selecting excerpts of text,

- using portions of text rewritten by English-speaking students,

- reading along with tape-recorded segments of text,

- using text re-presentations (see scaffolds below), and

- utilizing supplemental materials described above.

Integration

Integrating and organizing materials helps students make connections with various content areas and clarifies concepts and language.

Refer to page 91 for more information regarding the integrated curriculum.

Remember how hard your first day of algebra seemed? You barely understood, but were able to do the work with help. That night, however, you struggled to independently do your homework.

The classroom instruction was within your zone ("with help") but you were not yet able to work independently (beyond the zone). By the end of the semester, that first day's work became easy (independent or "known").

"You use the voices of others to guide you... until you can use your own voice as the guide."

—*Aida Walqui-van Lier*

The idea of sheltering instruction is supported by Vygotsky's (1978) idea of focusing instruction at a level that is just beyond students' independent ability level, but not so far off that learning is unattainable. This "zone of proximal development" as Vygotsky calls it, is the students' instructional level, or, the level at which students can function with help. This is where teachers should focus instruction that will move students forward in learning and conceptual development. As Aida Walqui-van Lier said, learning within the zone of proximal development means, "You use the voices of others to guide you... until you can use your own voice as the guide."

Sheltering strategies such as scaffolding provide the support (or help) English learners need to access the grade-level content at increasingly higher levels.

Teaching and Learning Zones

Good teachers, then, teach just beyond what students already know.

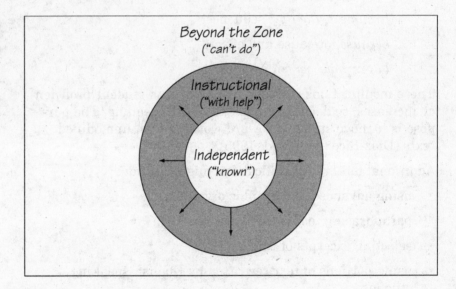

‘⊙ Strategies for SDAIE

Providing Comprehensible Input

HOW TO Techniques for providing comprehensible input, such as providing visuals and realia and modifying speech, are all equally useful for the SDAIE classroom. Refer to page 32 for a list of these techniques.

Using Scaffolds

HOW TO Scaffolds are strategies that support students' building of their own understanding (Walqui-van Lier, 1993). They refer to the visual or auditory supports supplied to the learners that enable them to participate in problem solving activities from the very beginning. The use of scaffolding, in essence, enables students to develop understanding (within the zone) that would otherwise be beyond their independent capacity (Faltis, 1993). Aida Walqui-van Lier (1993) identifies and describes the following scaffolds.

Identify ways in which you have used or can use the following scaffolds to help students access core curriculum:

Modeling

Modeling, or demonstrating, provides students with a clear picture of what is expected. The extra-linguistic clues clarify directions and provide concrete examples of the finished product. Any task that is introduced for the first time should be modeled.

Modeling

Bridging

Activating prior knowledge serves to establish the basis for new information. Tapping into prior knowledge or experience provides a personal link that demonstrates the relevance of the new material to students' lives, linking the known to the unknown. Bridging is accomplished in a variety of ways including brainstorming, developing anticipatory charts (graphic organizers), and identifying related literature, resources, or experiences.

Bridging

Contextualization

Teachers cannot rely on words alone to convey meaning. Words must be embedded in context to bring meaning to life. It is this context that helps students construct meaning of largely unfamiliar words. Using visuals, manipulatives, video clips, graphic organizers, and other realia (real stuff), serves to contextualize language and thereby promote understanding.

Contextualization

Schema Building

Schema building involves bringing to light the connections that exist between and across concepts and the curriculum. Students may not automatically make these connections. Using strategies such as advance organizers, graphic organiz-

Schema Building

ers, story mapping, jigsaw projects, etc., students gain a wider perspective regarding how concepts fit together, and how they may fit in the larger "scheme of things."

Metacognitive Development

Metacognitive Development

Metacognitive development involves the explicit teaching and learning of strategies that enable students to become autonomous learners. This conscious development of strategies and accompanying skills enables students to tackle academic tasks at increasingly higher levels. CALLA, reciprocal teaching, K-W-L activities, think-alouds, and directed reading-thinking, are examples of such strategies.

Text Re-presentation

Text Re-presentation

Text re-presentation involves taking a known (previously read) text and manipulating it for a new purpose. For example, summarizing a story or chapter, writing captions to capture the main ideas, writing an "eye-witness" account of an historical event, or developing collaborative posters or dialogs. This re-presentation of text allows students to use familiar text and then practice and extend writing to a new genre and for a new purpose.

Sheltered (or SDAIE) instruction is often viewed as simply "good teaching." However, *while these are good teaching strategies for all students, they are* **essential** *for English learners.*

Teachers of English learners must continually build scaffolds of understanding and support, as the needs arise. Conceptual development may take longer for English learners (as they are also acquiring language) and the teacher may not be able to cover as much detailed content.

Core concepts are developed by redistributing materials, and identifying areas of emphasis, resulting in a greater *depth* of learning. As Aida Walqui-van Lier (1993) puts it,

We may have "covered" less, but in the end, we will have "uncovered" more.

Using The Cognitive Academic Language Learning Approach (CALLA)

As the Natural Approach (introduced on page 37) and TPR (page 38) are approaches that promote the acquisition of language *fluency* (BICS), CALLA is a strategy that promotes the acquisition of *academic* language *proficiency* (CALP). It has long been noted that English learners who appear quite fluent still require additional assistance in achieving academic success in English. CALLA is an approach that focuses *explicitly* on teaching students strategies that will then equip them to become autonomous learners. These strategies empower students to achieve academically.

Refer to page 22 for a review of BICS and CALP.

CALLA integrates:

* *Content*—key concepts and ideas from core curriculum,

* *Language*—the language needed to access the content, and

* *Strategies*—the special techniques students apply and use on their own to help them learn.

It is the focus on the explicit development of learning strategies that is unique to CALLA.

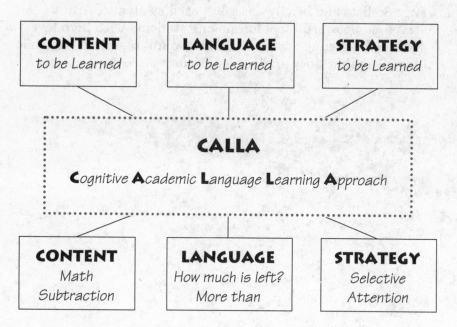

The CALLA Model

The CALLA model for academic language learning was developed by Anna Uhl Chamot and J. Michael O'Malley.

Review the CALLA strategies on page 85. Identify the strategies you use to:

- plan a lesson.
- plan a vacation/trip.
- learn the lyrics of a song.

Anna Uhl Chamot and J. Michael O'Malley, the creators of CALLA (1986), surveyed students from various language backgrounds to determine what they did that enabled them to achieve academically. They found that these achievers utilized strategies that helped them learn in school. Chamot and O'Malley classified the strategies under three headings:

Metacognitive Strategies

Metacognitive are those strategies that helped students think about, plan, monitor, and evaluate learning.

Cognitive Strategies

Cognitive strategies helped students as they were engaged in the learning process. They involve interacting with and/or manipulating the material mentally or physically, and applying a specific technique to the learning task.

Social Affective Strategies

Social Affective strategies helped students interact with another person, accomplish a task, or assisted in learning.

It was realized that these strategies could be explicitly taught. Once students have a working knowledge of each, they can employ them at will as the need arises. The teaching of these *learning strategies* became the framework for CALLA.

Page 85 lists and briefly describes each strategy. CALLA serves as a powerful tool for moving students with high levels of English language proficiency toward full cognitive academic language proficiency and academic success.

BRAINSTORM What are the three strategies you think your students should know immediately? Why?

CALLA Learning Strategies

Metacognitive Strategies

Advance Organization
Previewing the main ideas and concepts of the material to be learned, often by skimming the text for the organizing principle.

Advance Preparation
Rehearsing the language needed for an oral or written task.

Organizational Planning
Planning the parts, sequence, and main ideas to be expressed orally or in writing.

Selective Attention
Attending to, or scanning, key words, phrases, linguistic markers, sentences, or types of information.

Self-Evaluation
Judging how well one has accomplished a learning activity after it has been completed.

Cognitive Strategies

Contextualization
Placing a word or phrase in a meaningful sentence or category.

Elaboration
Relating new information to what is already known.

Grouping
Classifying words, terminology, or concepts according to their attributes.

Imagery
Using visual images (either mental or actual) to understand and remember new information.

Inferencing
Using information in the text to guess meanings of new items, predict outcomes, or complete missing parts.

Note-Taking
Writing down key words and concepts in abbreviated form during a listening or reading activity.

Resourcing
Using reference materials such as dictionaries, encyclopedias, or textbooks.

Summarizing
Making a mental or written summary of information gained through listening or reading.

Transfer
Using what is already known to facilitate a learning task.

Social Affective Strategies

Cooperation
Working together with peers to solve a problem, pool information, check a learning task, or get feedback on oral or written performance.

Questioning for Clarification
Eliciting from a teacher or peer additional explanation, rephrasing, or examples.

Self-Talk
Reducing anxiety by using mental techniques that make one feel competent to do the learning task.

From *The CALLA Handbook: Implementing the Cognitive Academic Language Learning Approach* by Anna Uhl Chamot and J. Michael O'Malley, © 1994. Reprinted by permission of Addison-Wesley Publishing Company.

Using Cooperative/Collaborative Learning

Cooperative learning...structures talk around content, requiring that students develop improved skills in thinking, and in language, in order to explain, persuade, encourage, disagree, inform, discuss, and negotiate. It provides ideal opportunities for second-language learners to hear and practice English beyond social language.

—Meyers, 1993

HOW TO
Cooperative and collaborative learning requires students to interact and rely on others and themselves to accomplish a task. These interactions may be structured formally, with each student assigned a specific and defined role in the group, or informally, with students collaborating to accomplish the task. When small groups of students collaborate on a common task, they must clarify and negotiate meaning with one another. This interactive exchange of information and ideas provides a rich language learning opportunity for English learners.

The cooperative learning environment offers many other rewards. Learners become more active, self-directed, and communicative. Academic achievement as well as discipline often improves as students experience success and take an active interest in what they are doing.

In addition, many English learners come from home cultures that value cooperation, sharing, and group achievement. A cooperative classroom is a particularly affirming environment for these children.

Many resources are available to help teachers fully utilize cooperative learning in all subject areas (Kagen, 1986; Johnson and Johnson, 1985). Mary Meyers (1993) identifies four major principles of cooperative learning:

1. Cooperative tasks are structured so that no one individual can complete the learning task alone.

2. Positive interdependence is fostered and developed. Students are evaluated individually and as a group.

3. Students work in different teams. Teams can be of three types: interest groups, random selection, or heterogeneous teams. The team configuration depends on the complexity, duration, and purpose of the task. Students are given opportunities to participate in a variety of groups.

4. Students learn both social and language skills necessary for cooperation at the same time as they learn content/concepts.

Tip This type of interactive learning is particularly helpful for English learners as it provides meaningful opportunities to use English in varied contexts, with varied English speakers, for varied purposes.

The following cooperative learning strategies or "structures" are particularly helpful with English learners. It is helpful to post the procedures for common structures on chart paper so groups can refer to the process as they work.

Brainstorming

Brainstorming can be accomplished with the whole class or a small group. The key is that all ideas are valid and recorded. Information from brainstorming can later be organized and categorized for easy use and retrieval.

Think-Pair-Share

This strategy has three components. Students are asked to:

- *Think:* Think carefully about the question (and answer).
- *Pair:* Find a partner.
- *Share:* Share answers with a partner, and prepare to share both answers with the entire class.

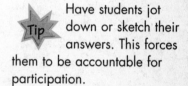
Tip Have students jot down or sketch their answers. This forces them to be accountable for participation.

Numbered Heads

For numbered heads, students work in groups of four, as follows:

- Students number themselves from one to four.
- The teacher asks a discussion question.
- Each group discusses the question and develops a team answer. Each member of the team must be able to answer the question.
- The teacher calls a number. The member from each team with the corresponding number raises a hand to respond. The teacher selects one "number X" to respond.

Novel Ideas

Novel ideas is used in conjunction with other structures. It may be used with partners or small groups.

- Students brainstorm and list ideas or answers to a question.
- Groups take turns sharing their list. Each group may name only the ideas or answers that have not previously been mentioned.
- Students must listen attentively and eliminate common answers from their lists, responding with *novel ideas only*.

Round Robin

The Round Robin strategy has students take turns sharing ideas, giving answers, or adding information. No one interrupts. All have a turn.

Jigsaw

Also called expert groups, jigsaw is a four-step structure.

- Step One: Students form a "home" group of three to five.

- Step Two: Students number off. Each member is responsible for mastering one part of the assignment.

- Step Three: Students move to form an "expert" group with students from other groups with the same number. (For example, all 1s, 2s, etc.) This expert group completes their assigned part of the task, and each of its members is capable of teaching the information.

- Step Four: Students return to their home groups. Each expert shares (or teaches) the content learned in the expert group with the members of the home group.

Using Graphic Organizers

HOW TO Graphic organizers are tools that help to visually organize information. They are useful across the curriculum, from developing basic vocabulary, to identifying and synthesizing elements of literature, to processing information in core content areas. There is some evidence to show that graphic organizers actually help the brain to store and process information more efficiently. Graphic organizers are particularly useful in aiding comprehension for English learners as they serve to visually represent, organize, and contextualize language.

Refer to the facing page for varied examples of graphic organizers.

More examples of story maps, a form of graphic organizer, are illustrated in Chapter 3, pages 66–68.

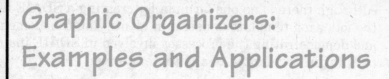

Graphic Organizers: Examples and Applications

KWL

What I KNOW	What I WANT to know	What I LEARNED

Background Knowledge/Evaluate Learning

VENN DIAGRAM

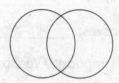

Comparing/Contrasting

ANTICIPATORY/INPUT CHART

True	False	Statement
		▬▬▬▬▬▬▬

Background/Prior Knowledge

CLUSTER

Brainstorming/Organizing Information

WEB

Analyzing Attributes

T-CHART

Looks Like	Sounds Like

Visualizing/Comparing Attributes

PICTORIAL INPUT

Building Vocabulary and Background

VOCABULARY CHART

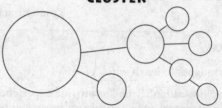

Three Little Pigs

1. pigs
2. straw

Visualizing/Building Vocabulary

MATRIX/PROCESS GRID

Animal	Body Covering	Backbone
snake		
dog		

Classifying/Comparing Information

SEQUENCE OF EVENTS CHAIN

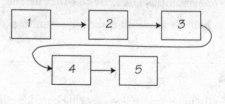

Visually Sequencing Events

Use the format to outline a SDAIE lesson for English learners. Include the strategies and activities you would include in each step. A blank template is provided on page 107.

Although there is no one formula for creating a SDAIE lesson, the following template is useful in identifying the elements and demonstrating the processes involved in SDAIE instruction. It can be adapted to any content area.

Lesson Topic/Title: _____

Learning Objectives: _____

Key Concepts/Language/Vocabulary to Develop:

    Content Obligatory: The language and vocabulary that directly relates to the content to be learned.

    Content Supportive: The language and vocabulary used in the lesson that supports the content activity in terms of process, procedure, etc.

Introduce

Prepare students to learn with:

- *Experiences:* Identify and/or provide experiences that focus students. Provide experiences such as poems, music, literature, guest speakers, experiments, video, film, or field trips.

- *Prior Knowledge:* Tap into and connect prior knowledge to current learning. Determine what students already know and identify misconceptions. Utilize brainstorming, KWL charts, or other graphic organizers.

Explore

Provide relevant instruction and practice through:

- *Presentation:* Present information and develop concepts utilizing strategies that are appropriate to the content and English proficiency levels of the students.

  Utilize SDAIE strategies (e.g., scaffolds, graphic organizers, and cooperative/collaborative learning) and appropriate tools, materials, and resources. Modify materials and presentation to enhance comprehension and learning.

- *Practice:* Allow students opportunities to work independently, with partners, and in collaborative/cooperative groups. Ensure that students are clear about the process and purpose of the activity.

Utilize varied grouping configurations and activities that appeal to a variety of learning styles. Monitor students, providing feedback, direction, and guidance as needed.

Extend

Provide opportunities and activities that extend, enrich, and integrate learning across the curriculum.

Focus on helping students make important conceptual and linguistic connections across the curriculum.

Assess

Continually monitor students by checking for clarification, observing concept and skill development, and modifying instruction to match student needs (ongoing assessment). In addition, determine the degree to which students have achieved the objectives of the lesson.

Integrating the Curriculum

Language and content are best learned within meaningful contexts. Integrating the curriculum provides this context and serves to efficiently develop and connect seemingly diverse concepts and ideas, and develop the language that embodies them.

Integrated instruction also helps to manage the multi-level classroom. For example, the classroom is organized around a broad theme. Individual students or groups explore various topics (specific subsets of the theme) that are suited to their needs, interests, and abilities. Classroom resources, bulletin boards, field trips, art projects, and other activities emerge from the theme. The teacher can modify instructional activities to match the needs and interests of each group.

Integrated instruction for English learners can be viewed in two ways:

- Integrated English language development, and
- Integrated curriculum program.

Integrated English Language Development

As discussed in Chapter 2, a balanced English language development program includes activities characterized as literature, content, or communications based (in addition to integrating listening, speaking, reading, writing, and higher-order thinking skills into these activities). The "core" lesson is enriched and extended by tying in related context area experiences. The primary purpose or goal of these content extensions is English language development. Content serves as the vehicle (much like content-based ELD).

Page 92 provides an example of an Integrated ELD unit. Its focus is a literature piece titled "Only a Nickel." Note the content extensions for the literary selection.

> **Tip** Brainstorm extension activities for another piece of literature or topic. Use the web template on page 105 to record the information.

Integrated Curriculum Program

An integrated program involves integrating the entire instructional day around a specific theme. It has added requirements that provide structure and guidance. These requirements include:

- Identifying and incorporating the grade-level goals and objectives for each curricular area,
- Organizing instruction and using appropriate strategies so that the individual academic and linguistic needs of all students are met,
- Identifying and gathering resources and materials to support the theme.

Literature Web

Reading
- Shared reading of the Big Books
- Individual reading of the Little Book
- Buddy reading aloud (in pairs)
- Read for details
- Cloze exercise
- Conventions of print
- Phonics

Music
- Listen to tape
- Create original new verses to song "Yummy Yummy"
- Create fairground noises
- Other music about animals, the country, food, money
- Make instruments that bang/whee/ring, etc.

Math
- Money concepts
- Counting and comparing
- Math stories
- Problem solving
- Classroom shopping
- Recipes—measuring, sequencing, sorting.

Listening
- To the story read aloud
- To the cassette tape
- To classroom plays
- Collaborative groups
- Pair-work

ONLY A NICKEL

Science
- Basic food groups; favorite foods
- Metals—nickel, copper, silver
- Recipes—solids/liquids
- Fairground rides (motion)
- Animals: in story, favorite, wild vs. tame, habitats, real food
- Seasons

Writing
- New song verses
- New stories
- Descriptions of illustrations
- Recipes
- Sequels/prequels

Social Studies
- Country vs. city environment
- State fairs—what to see/do
- Multicultural celebrations

Thinking Speaking
- Predict the story
- Summarize the story
- Answer reference and display questions
- Retell the story in L1 and L2
- Language usage—adjectives/rhyming words
- Describe illustrations
- Roleplay

Art
- Masks or props for performances
- Collaborative mural of fair as backdrop for classroom fair
- Food booths—ice cream, popcorn, etc.
- Game booths—can toss, ring the bottles, duck shoots
- Illustrate new stories

Drama
- Reader's theater—groups of 3
- Mime story
- Create parts for "non-speaking" animals in art
- Write new plays

In an integrated program, the theme serves as an organizing tool. The purpose of an integrated program is to develop grade-level core curriculum (much like SDAIE) in a way that helps students utilize the natural connections between the disciplines.

The more simplified or "informal" integration that occurs within an integrated ELD program can serve as the basic structure or format for the more extensive integrated program.

Integrating curriculum, in either case, is more than simply correlating topics. It is the careful integration of broad themes, or "big ideas," that help students make connections. Few problems in life are solved simply by applying knowledge from one distinct discipline. When students learn through thematic units:

- They become familiar with the general context.

- New information is easy to introduce. It relates directly to the familiar, making it more meaningful.

- The brain seems to search for meaning through patterns and patterning.

- A powerful integrated learning environment is established where students are better able to assimilate new, but related information.

- Language is facilitated because theme-related language and vocabulary are used and reused in new and varying contexts, all of which are meaningfully related (Ford, 1995).

Teaching Strategies Checklist

The checklist on the next page outlines some of the most important behaviors necessary in providing meaningful instruction for English learners. Review the behaviors and reflect on the successful teaching experiences you have had or viewed.

Tip Wise teachers point out that the theme must serve learning (not vice-versa). Effective teachers dip in and out of the overarching class theme, bringing deeper meaning, insight, and skill to the big ideas and specific content areas. Side-trips, however, are occasionally made as needed.

Tip With a partner, use the checklist on page 94 to observe and record the teaching behaviors each of you use. Reflect on and discuss the completed checklist. Identify the areas that are your strengths, as well as those areas that need improvement.

Strategies for Teaching English Learners: Observation Checklist

Teacher _____ Date _____

School _____ Observer _____

Grade Level _____ Lesson Observed _____

Number of Students _____ Start _____ Finish _____

A. Comprehensible Input and Output

	Observed	Not observed	Not applicable
1. Uses contextual references (visuals, realia).	❑	❑	❑
2. Implements listening activities to assist students in developing the sounds of English.	❑	❑	❑
3. Allows for an initial listening (or "silent") period for students at the pre-production level.	❑	❑	❑
4. Uses a variety of questioning strategies and activities to meet the needs of individuals at varying stages of language acquisition.	❑	❑	❑
5. Exposes students to higher levels of comprehensible language (i+1).	❑	❑	❑
6. Links new vocabulary and language to previously learned information.	❑	❑	❑
7. Provides activities and opportunities for increased student talk as students develop English.	❑	❑	❑
8. Taps into and accesses students' prior knowledge.	❑	❑	❑

B. Negotiation of Meaning

	Observed	Not observed	Not applicable
1. Monitors student comprehension through interactive means such as checking for comprehension and clarification, utilizing questioning strategies, having students paraphrase, define, and model.	❑	❑	❑
2. Modifyies instruction as needed using strategies such as scaffolding, expansion, demonstration, and modeling.	❑	❑	❑
3. Encourages students to communicate in English, using familiar vocabulary and structures.	❑	❑	❑
4. Modifies teacher-talk to make input comprehensible.	❑	❑	❑
5. Uses extra-linguistic clues (e.g., gestures, facial expressions) to emphasize or clarify meaning.	❑	❑	❑
6. Matches language with experience.	❑	❑	❑
7. Models the language with natural speech and intonation.	❑	❑	❑
8. Provides opportunities for students to use English with varied audiences and for a variety of purposes.	❑	❑	❑
9. Verifies that all students comprehend before moving on.	❑	❑	❑

Comments: _____

_____

_____

C. "Sheltered" Content Instruction

	Observed	Not observed	Not applicable
1. Modifies the language input according to the needs of the students (e.g., rate of speech, added definitions and examples, controlled vocabulary, and careful use of idioms).	❑	❑	❑
2. Reviews main topic and key vocabulary and ideas.	❑	❑	❑
3. Checks frequently for understanding.			
4. Bridges new "unknown" material to "known"—what students have already learned.	❑	❑	❑
5. Organizes instruction around themes and content appropriate to students' grade level.	❑	❑	❑
6. Engages students in active participation activities and responses.	❑	❑	❑
7. Integrates culture and content instruction.	❑	❑	❑
8. Uses added resources and strategies to help students access core curriculum.	❑	❑	❑

D. Thinking Skills

	Observed	Not observed	Not applicable
1. Asks questions, gives directions, and generates activities to advance students to higher levels of thinking (from recalling to evaluating).	❑	❑	❑
2. Elicits student questions and encourages them to support their answers.	❑	❑	❑
3. Allows ample wait time after asking questions.	❑	❑	❑
4. Guides students through learning using varied groupings and configurations.	❑	❑	❑

E. Error Correction

	Observed	Not observed	Not applicable
1. Practices sensitive error correction, focusing on errors of meaning rather than form.	❑	❑	❑
2. Accepts appropriate student responses.	❑	❑	❑
3. Encourages taking risks in English.	❑	❑	❑
4. Develops classroom activities to address recurring or systematic errors.	❑	❑	❑
5. Allows for flow of uninterrupted student thought.	❑	❑	❑

F. Classroom Climate

	Observed	Not observed	Not applicable
1. Uses relevant material.	❑	❑	❑
2. Displays of student work are evident.	❑	❑	❑
3. Utilizes (and demonstrates respect for) students' home language and culture.	❑	❑	❑
4. Nurtures a positive climate.	❑	❑	❑
5. Rewards all attempts at language.	❑	❑	❑

THE AMAZING ENGLISH! HOW-TO HANDBOOK

▲ Review: Academic/Content Area Development

Refer to and review the preview page for this chapter on page 73.

Was your prior knowledge accurate? (Did you have any misconceptions or inaccurate ideas?)

What did you LEARN about academic/content area development?

How can you apply this information? (Include 1-2 specific ideas.)

What else would you want to know?

Assessment and Evaluation

Assessment has many purposes: to diagnose strengths and weaknesses, prescribe instruction and approaches, screen and select participants, identify placement and progress, evaluate the effectiveness of a program, and assess attitudes. Clearly, the assessment methods and tools must match the purpose of assessment.

This chapter will focus on assessment as a means of reflecting the thinking of the student, and the student's ability to effectively communicate that thinking in all of the English language domains: listening, speaking, reading, and writing. Assessment will be viewed in terms of its:

- alignment with the authentic learning opportunities provided in the classroom,

- purpose in measuring what students can do, and

- value as a tool for evaluating student needs and designing further instructional activities.

Preview: Assessment and Evaluation

What do you already *KNOW* about assessment and evaluation?

What do you *WANT* to know or learn?

The Basic Principles of Assessment

Assessment of students takes on various forms. There are basic principles, however, that should be observed:

Child-Centered

Assessment should focus on student strengths: what they can do, what they know, and how they have grown and progressed as English learners.

Ongoing: Formative and Embedded

Assessment is a part of the daily activity of the classroom. It is embedded in the interactions teachers have with students. Checking for clarification, monitoring instruction to match student needs, and asking comprehension questions are all examples of ongoing assessment. This ongoing assessment can be informal, as in the above examples, or formal. Formal ongoing assessment entails measuring progress at regular intervals and documenting student growth over time. A variety of tools can be used, such as portfolios and established benchmarks and rubrics.

Summative

Summative evaluation tends to be more formal, assessing students after a specified period of time or after specific instructional activities. It is the summation of learning, reflecting what has already been monitored and evaluated over time.

Formal and Informal

Assessment runs along a continuum from informal (observations, anecdotal notes, clarification checks) to formal (testing instruments, performance tasks measured against a rubric). Formal and informal assessments have value and should be incorporated in a student's overall program.

Involves the Student, Teacher, and Parents

Opportunities for student self-assessment and a developing sense of personal responsibility for learning should be incorporated as a part of assessment. Additionally, parent involvement, including their perceptions of their children's strengths and talents, as well as their expectations and concerns about the school, will prove invaluable in providing appropriate assessment and instruction. Parents should be invited to conference and also examine assessment information, such as portfolios, on a regular basis.

Tip Encourage parents to identify their own observed areas of strength or interest. Use this information to design learning tasks that build on student strengths.

Varied

Providing a variety of assessment opportunities is important in order to get a complete picture of students' abilities and growth, as well as to avoid negative biases based on factors such as culture and learning styles.

HOW TO Providing a Variety of Assessment Opportunities

Assessment options range from standardized, skill-based instruments to more authentic assessment such as portfolios and performance-based assessments. To provide a complete evaluation of student progress, a variety of assessment materials and opportunities should be utilized.

Portfolio

Portfolio assessment is a focused, collaborative evaluation and analysis of the materials collected in a student's portfolio. The represented material is a meaningful collection of student work, gathered over time, that reflects learning with regard to instructional objectives (O'Malley and Valdez Pierce, 1996) and represents the student's efforts, achievements, and personal, academic, and linguistic growth. Portfolio contents will vary considerably depending on the individual teacher and student goals. In addition to student work, portfolios may also contain informative materials from students, teachers, or parents, such as anecdotal records, self-assessments, checklists, scoring rubrics, audio or video recordings of student activities, parent/student questionnaires, student reflections, and peer conference reports.

Student portfolios are an excellent tool for parent conferencing. Parents are able to see concrete examples of their child's progress and contribute information from their unique perspectives.

Observation

Student observations are done informally, while monitoring classroom work and participation, and can also be recorded on checklists or anecdotal records. "Kid-watching" is a powerful source of valuable information regarding what and how children are learning.

Performance Tasks

Performance tasks require students to apply learned information or concepts to accomplish a task. The degree to which the task is accomplished (sometimes measured against a bench-

Identify the types of assessment opportunities you have provided. Describe the purposes and circumstances of the assessments.

Tip Determine the criteria by which items will be included in the student portfolio. To aid in interpreting the portfolio, include a description of the circumstances under which the entries were originally developed and the degree to which the work achieved the expected standards.

Tip Watch for the conditions under which individuals seem to learn best. Keep this in mind as you plan instructional activities.

mark or rubric) forms the basis of the assessment. Performance tasks are valuable in that they demonstrate what students can do in relation to specified objectives or standards.

Self-Assessment

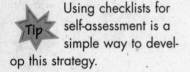
Using checklists for self-assessment is a simple way to develop this strategy.

As students reflect on and evaluate their own learning, they are developing a sense of personal responsibility and insight into their own strengths and talents. Accurate self-evaluation enhances self-esteem and promotes trust between teacher and student (Eisele, 1991).

Standardized/Skills Tests

Since most students will have to take standardized tests, it makes sense to prepare them for this task. Help students develop "test-taking" skills and strategies.

Standardized instruments are also sources of valuable assessment information. Such instruments help in gauging student progress both as a group and as individuals in relation to a group. Students should first receive instruction in strategies for taking such tests.

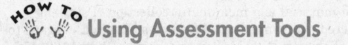

Using Assessment Tools

The following assessment tools are used independently and in varied combinations to supplement, reinforce, and validate the assessment processes described above.

Anecdotal Records

Use a clipboard and pages of adhesive labels. Write the observations on the labels, date them, and transfer them to the students' files.

Anecdotal records are descriptions of students' actions written as they occur or soon afterwards. The goal is to briefly transcribe what the child says or does and the context in which the behavior takes place. These accounts preserve a rich history of information about how a student learns and interacts in the school environment. In combination with portfolios and checklists, anecdotal records help teachers analyze a student's accomplishments and approach to learning over time.

Audio/Video Tapes

Taping what students actually do and say is an excellent means of documenting student behavior patterns and language development.

Logs or Journals

Student-produced learning logs or journals for reading, writing, or content learning serve to document students' language, literacy, and cognitive development and learning, as well as their ability to express this development and learning in informal, written forms. In addition, these tools serve to place reading and writing in a context that is functional and personally relevant. Students are often amazed to see their own growth and development over time.

Conferences

A conference is a time to meet and reflect on a student's work. It may involve the student, teacher, and the parent. The student can take the lead in the conference, choosing pieces of work to discuss. Parents and teachers can offer their own observations and insights about particular works. Conferences provide the forum for students and teachers to set new learning goals together. Parents can also have input into this process.

Checklists

Checklists are tools for organizing and visually identifying the accomplishments of students in relation to specific learning objectives, skills, and behaviors. They give clear answers to clear questions. Checklists help teachers to manage information related to content, learning, and individual progress and then easily use the information to assess and evaluate student needs.

Rubrics

A scoring rubric is a rating scale that identifies the degree to which a student has met a specified standard. It can be very discrete, relating to a specific task (writing a letter), or broad in scope (development of oral language proficiency). Rubrics are valuable in identifying visible behaviors or traits that serve to measure growth and progress toward specified goals or standards.

Standardized and Skills Tests

As mentioned above, standardized or skills tests can be useful in gauging students' progress both as a group and as individuals in relation to a group.

Tip Make sure students understand the purpose of a learning log or journal. (Its purpose may differ from daily writing or interactive journals.) Students should know that many people may be reading these journals.

Tip Use checklists to help assure a balanced program of concept, language, and skill development.

⟳ Evaluation: Making Judgments

Tip Schedule regular opportunities (or use reporting periods) to reflect and complete this important evaluative task. Evaluation is a powerful tool in guiding appropriate instruction.

A fundamental goal of assessment is to *inform instruction.* If we clearly observe what students know and can do, we can then understand what must be taught next (Fisette, 1993). Evaluation is the process of analyzing assessment information to make judgments about student performance and suggest improvements or instructional modifications. Effective evaluation should answer these questions:

- Where did the student begin?

- Where is the student going?

- Is the student finding success?

- If not, what changes should be made to meet student needs and ensure future success? (Eisele, 1991)

Using all assessment information—formal and informal, from portfolios to standardized and skills tests—provides balanced evaluation that conveys a more accurate picture of student progress. With this clear picture, teachers are then equipped to modify, enrich, and customize instruction that accurately meets students' needs and moves them toward the full accomplishment of established academic goals.

How do you provide for student evaluation?

Portfolio Assessment

Portfolio contents are one way to represent the student's linguistic achievements.

Review: Assessment and Evaluation

Refer to and review the preview page for this chapter on page 97.

Was your prior knowledge accurate? (Did you have any misconceptions or inaccurate ideas?)

What did you LEARN about assessment and evaluation?

How can you apply this information? (Include 1-2 specific ideas.)

What else would you want to know?

Resource Pages

Background Information Survey for English Language Learners

Name _____ Date _____

Address _____

_____

Home Phone: _____ Birth Date: _____

Primary Language: _____ Current Grade: _____

Age of Arrival (to USA): _____ Country of Origin: _____

Other circumstances of arrival:_____

_____

Family Background

Who lives at home? _____

What language(s) is most frequently spoken in the home? _____

Is there someone at home who speaks English? _____

Personal Background

Special interests, talents, or abilities?_____

_____

Health conditions/concerns? _____

_____

Previous Education

Years of previous schooling: _____ Where?_____

Language(s) of instruction:_____

Previous exposure to English: _____

Language Proficiency on Arrival

English Assessment:

Oral fluency:_____ Literacy: _____

Development of academic language (CALP): _____

Primary Language Assessment:

Oral Fluency_____ Literacy: _____

Development of academic language (CALP): _____

Parent/Information/Conference

Is there anything about your child, family, or culture that you want the school/teacher to know or understand? _____

_____

Web Template

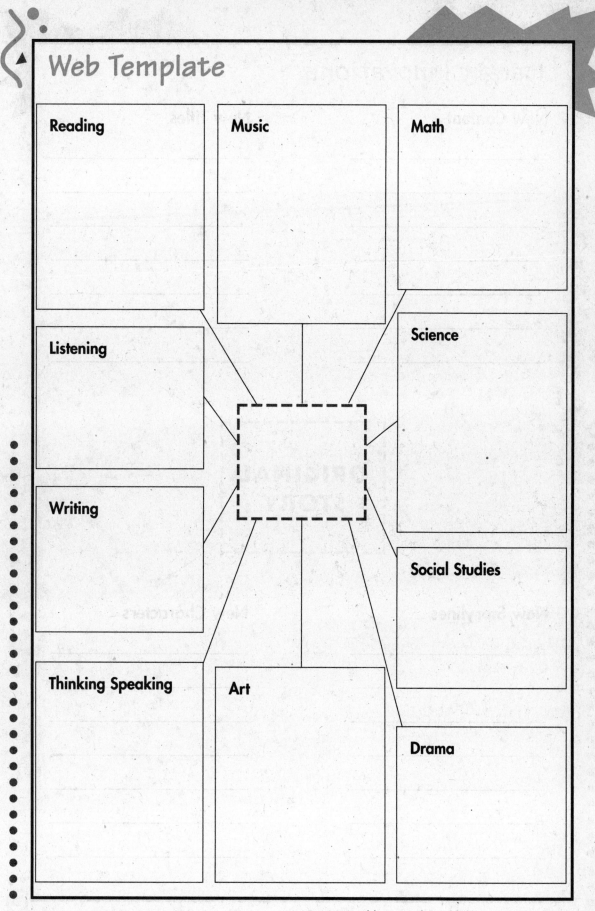

Reading

Music

Math

Listening

Science

Writing

Social Studies

Thinking Speaking

Art

Drama

Literary Innovations

New Content

_____

_____

_____

_____

_____

_____

New Titles

_____

_____

_____

_____

_____

_____

ORIGINAL STORY

New Storylines

_____

_____

_____

_____

_____

_____

New Characters

_____

_____

_____

_____

_____

_____

© 1996, Addison-Wesley Publishing Company, Inc.

Planning a SDAIE Lesson

Lesson Topic/Title: _____

Learning Objectives: _____

Key Concepts/Language/Vocabulary to Develop:

    Content Obligatory: _____

    _____

    Content Supportive: _____

    _____

Introduce	Materials
Explore	
Extend	
Assess	

References

References

Adams, M. and Bruck, M. (1995) "Learning to Read: Resolving the "Great Debate"." *American Federation of Teachers,* Summer, 1995.

Asher, J. (1982) *Learning Another Language Through Actions: The Complete Teachers' Guidebook.* Los Gatos, CA: Sky Oaks.

Atwell, N. (1987) *In the Middle: Writing, Reading, and Learning with Adolescents.* Portsmouth, NH: Heinemann.

Banks, James A. (1988) *Multiethnic Education: Theory and Practice, Second Edition.* Boston: Allyn and Bacon.

Bennett, Christine (1990) *Comprehensive Multicultural Education.* Boston: Allyn and Bacon.

Bogomaz, B. and McMillan, S. (1995) in *English Learner Achievement Project (ELAP) Training Handbook.* San Diego: San Diego City Schools.

California Department of Education (1992) *It's Elementary: Elementary Grades Task Force Report.* Sacramento: California State Department of Education.

California State Department of Education, Bilingual Education Office (1986) *Beyond Language: Social and Cultural Factors in Schooling Language Minority Students.* Los Angeles: California State University.

Calkins, L. (1991) *Living Between the Lines.* Portsmouth, NH: Heinemann.

Cambourne, B. (1988) *The Whole Story: Natural Learning and the Acquisition of Literacy in the Classroom.* Richmond Hill, Ontario: Scholastic-TAB.

Canale, M. (1983) "From Communicative Competence to Communicative Language Pedagogy." In J. Richards and Schmidt (Eds.), *Language and Communication.* New York: Longman.

Chamot, A. U. and O'Malley, J. M. (1986) *A Cognitive Academic Language Learning Approach: An ESL Content-based Curriculum.* Washington, D.C.: National Clearinghouse for Bilingual Education.

Chamot, A. U. and O'Malley, J. M. (1987) "The Cognitive Academic Language Learning Approach: A Bridge to the Mainstream." *TESOL Quarterly,* 21(2): 238.

Chamot, A. U. and O'Malley, J. M. (1994) *The CALLA Handbook: Implementing the Cognitive Academic Language Learning Approach.* Reading, MA: Addison-Wesley.

Chesterfield, R. and Chesterfield, K. (1985) "Natural Order In Children's Use Of Second Language Learning Strategies." *Applied Linguistics,* 6: 45-59.

THE AMAZING ENGLISH! HOW-TO HANDBOOK

Collier, V. (1987) "Age and Rate of Acquisition of Second Language for Academic Purposes." *TESOL Quarterly*, 21(4): 617-641.

Cummins, J. (1984) *Bilingualism and Special Education: Issues in Assessment and Pedagogy*. San Diego: College-Hill.

Cummins, J. (1989) *Empowering Minority Students*. Sacramento: California Association for Bilingual Education.

Cummins, J. (1993) *The Acquisition of English as a Second Language*. Presentation article/handout for California Elementary Education Association, San Diego.

Cummins, J. (1981) "The Role of Primary Language Development in Promoting Educational Success for Language Minority Students." In *Schooling and Language Minority Students: A Theoretical Framework*. Sacramento: California State Department of Education.

Denton, D. (1988) *Whole Language: The Beginning... The Middle... Never Ending!* Handout presented at Longfellow Elementary, San Diego, CA.

Diaz-Rico, L. and Weed, K. (1995) *The Crosscultural, Language, and Academic Development Handbook*. Needham Heights, MA: Allyn and Bacon.

Eisele, Beverly (1991) *Managing the Whole Language Classroom*. Cypress: Creative Teaching Press.

Enright, D. and McCloskey, M. (1988) *Integrating English: Developing English Language and Literacy in the Multilingual Classroom*. Reading, MA: Addison-Wesley.

Faltis, C. (1993) *JOINFOSTERING: Adapting Teaching Strategies for the Multilingual Classroom*. New York: Macmillan.

Freeman, Y. and Freeman, D. (1992) *Whole Language for Second Language Learners*. Portsmouth, NH: Heinemann.

Fisette, D. (1993) "Practical Authentic Assessment: Good Kid Watchers Know What to Teach Next!" *The California Reader,* Summer, 26(4): 4-9.

Fisher, B. (1995) "We *Do* Teach Phonics." *Teaching K-8,* September.

Gardner, H. (1985) *Frames of Mind: The Theory of Multiple Intelligences*. New York: HarperCollins.

Gibbons, P. (1993) *Learning to Learn in a Second Language*. Portsmouth, NH: Heinemann.

Goodman, K. (1968). "The Psycholinguistic Nature of the Reading Process." In *The Psycholinguistic Nature of the Reading Process,* K. Goodman, ed. Detroit: Wayne State University Press, 13-26.

References

Goodman, K. (1986) *What's Whole in Whole Language.* Portsmouth, N.H.: Heinemann.

Goodman, K., Goodman Y., and Hood, W. (1989) *The Whole Language Evaluation Book.* Portsmouth, N.H.: Heinemann.

Haggerty, Brian (1995) *Nurturing Intelligences: A Guide to Multiple Intelligence Theory and Teaching.* Reading: Addison-Wesley.

Haggerty, Brian (1996) *Nurturing Intelligences: Core Literature Series: Teaching Guide to Russel Freedman's Lincoln: A Photobiography.* Reading: Addison-Wesley.

Heald-Taylor, Gail (1991) *Whole Language Strategies for ESL Students.* San Diego: Dominie Press.

Holdaway, D. (1979) *The Foundations of Literacy.* Portsmouth, NH: Heinemann.

Holdaway, D. (1986) in *The Pursuit of Literacy: Early Reading and Writing,* Michael Sampson (ed.). Kendall/Hunt Publishing.

Honig, B. (1995) *How Should We Teach Our Children To Read? A Balanced Approach.* (Pre-publication draft).

Hymes, D. (1974) *Directions in Sociolinguistics.* Philadelphia: University of Pennsylvania Press.

Johnson, D.W. and Johnson, R.T. (1885) *Structuring Cooperative Learning: Lesson Plans for Teachers.* Edina, MN: Interaction Book Company.

Johnson, D.W., Johnson, R.T., and Holubec, E.J. (1986) *Circles of Learning: Cooperation in the Classroom, Revised.* Edina, MN: Interaction Book Company.

Johnson, T. and Louis, D. (1987) *Literacy Through Literature.* Portsmouth: Heinemann.

Kagen, S. (1986) "Cooperative Learning and Sociocultural Factors in Schooling." In *Beyond Language: Social and Cultural Factors in Schooling Language Minority Students.* Sacramento: California State Department of Education.

Krashen, S. (1981) "Bilingual Education and Second Language Acquisition Theory." In *Schooling and Language Minority Students: A Theoretical Framework.* Sacramento: California State Department of Education.

Krashen, S. (1993) *The Power of Reading.* Englewood, CO: Libraries Unlimited.

Krashen, S. and Terrell, T. (1983) *The Natural Approach.* Hayward: The Alemany Press.

Krashen, S., Long, M., and Scarcella, R. (1979) "Age, Rate, and Eventual Attainment in Second Language Acquisition." *TESOL Quarterly,* 13(4): 573-582.

Lapp, D., Flood, J., and Tinajero, J. (1994) "Are We Communicating? Effective Instruction for Students Who Are Acquiring English as a Second Language." *The Reading Teacher*, 48 (3): 260-264.

Law, B. and Eckes, M. (1990) *The More Than Just Surviving Handbook: ESL for Every Classroom Teacher*. Winnipeg, Canada: Penguin.

Long, M. (1982) "Input, Interaction, and Second Language Acquisition." *TESOL Quarterly*, 207-225.

Long, M. and Crookes G. (1992) "Three Approaches to Task-Based Syllabus Design." *TESOL Quarterly*, 27-56.

McMillan, S. (1995) in *English Learner Achievement Project (ELAP) Training Handbook*. San Diego: San Diego City Schools.

Meyers, Mary (1993) *Teaching to Diversity: Teaching and Learning in the Multi-ethnic Classroom*. Toronto: Irwin Publishing. (U.S. Edition, Reading: Addison-Wesley).

Mooney, M. (1995) "Guided Reading Beyond the Primary Grades." *Teaching K-8*, September; *Instructor*, July/August.

Mooney, M. (1990) *Reading To, With, and By Children*. Katonah, NY: Richard Owen Publishers.

Nelson, K. (1995) "Nurturing Kids' Seven Ways of Being Smart." *Instructor*, July/August.

Olsen, L. and Chen, T. (1988) *The World Enrolls*. San Francisco: California Tomorrow.

O'Malley, J.M. and Valdez Pierce, L. (1996) *Authentic Assessment for English Language Learners: Practical Strategies for Teachers*. Reading, MA: Addison-Wesley.

Ramirez, J. (1992) "Executive Summary, Final Report: Longitudinal Study of Structured Immersion Strategy, Early-Exit and Late-Exit Transitional Bilingual Education Programs for Language-Minority Children." *Bilingual Research Journal*, 16 (1, 2): 1–62.

Richard-Amato, P. (1988) *Making it Happen*. White Plains, NY: Longman.

Richard-Amato, P. and Marguerite Ann Snow, eds. (1992) *The Multicultural Classroom*. White Plains, NY: Longman.

Routman, R. (1988, 1991) *Invitations*. Portsmouth, NH: Heinemann.

Rubin, J. (1975) "What the Good Language Learner Can Teach Us." *TESOL Quarterly*, 9: 41-51.

Rubin, J. and Thompson, I. (1982) *How to be a More Successful Language Learner*. Boston: Heinle and Heinle.

Schell, E. (1995) *"The Workshop Approach to Reading, Writing, and History."* In *English Learner Achievement Project (ELAP) Training Handbook*. San Diego: San Diego City Schools.

Skutnabb-Kangas, T. (1984) *Bilingualism or Not: The Education of Minorities*. Clevedon: Multilingual Matters.

Smith, F. (1988) *Joining the Literacy Club: Further Essays into Education*. Portsmouth, NH: Heinemann.

Smith, F. (1971) *Understanding Reading*. Toronto: Holt-Rinehart & Winston.

Sobul, D. (1994) *"Strategies to Meet the Goals of SDAIE."* Presentation at California Association of Bilingual Education, San Jose.

Sweet, A. (1993) *State of the Art: Transforming Ideas for Teaching and Learning to Read*. Washington DC: US Department of Education, US Government Printing Office.

Terrell, T. (1981) "The Natural Approach in Bilingual Education." In *Schooling and Language Minority Students: A Theoretical Framework*. Sacramento: California State Department of Education.

Thoele, S. Patton (1991) "Making a Difference." In *The Woman's Book of Courage*. Conari Press.

Tiedt, P. and Tiedt, I. (1979) *Multicultural Teaching: A Handbook of Activities, Information, and Resources*. Boston: Allyn and Bacon.

Tinajero, J. and Calderon, M. (1988) "Language Experience Approach Plus." *Journal of Educational Issues of Language Minority Students*, 2: 31-45.

Traill, Leanna (1989) "Classroom Environment and Organization." Presentation handout.

Treadway, J. (1989) "The Directed Reading-Thinking Activity." *Learning Magazine,* April: 56-57.

Treadway, J. (1995) *Directed Reading-Thinking Activities*. Presentation at Mann Middle School, San Diego.

Van Allen, R. (1973) "The Language Experience Approach." In R. Karlen (ed.) *Perspectives on Elementary Reading: Principles and Strategies of Teaching*. New York: Harcourt Brace Jovanovich.

Vygotsksy, L.S. (1978) *Mind in Society*. Cambridge, MA: Harvard University Press.

Walqui-van Lier, A. (1993) "Sheltered Instruction: Doing it Right." In *Bilingual Teacher Training Program: Sheltered Instruction Institute*. San Diego: San Diego County Office of Education.

Walqui-van Lier, A. (1993) "Literature Review: Sheltered Instruction." In *Bilingual Teacher Training Program: Sheltered Instruction Institute*. San Diego: San Diego County Office of Education.

Walter, T. (1995) in *English Learner Achievement Project (ELAP) Training Handbook*. San Diego: San Diego City Schools.

Willis, S. (1995) "Whole Language, Finding the Surest Way to Literacy." *Curriculum Update*. (Fall 1995) Alexandria, VA: Association for Supervision and Curriculum Development.

Wong Fillmore, L. (1991) "Second Language Learning in Children: A Model of Language Learning in a Social Context." In E. Bialystok (ed.) *Language Processing In Bilingual Children*. Cambridge: Cambridge University Press, 49-69.

Yorio, C. (1980) "The Teacher's Attitude Toward the Student's Output in the Second Language Classroom." *CATESOL Occasional Papers, California Association of Teachers of English to Speakers of Other Languages,* November 1-8.